Solon W. Pierce

Battle Fields and Camp Fires of the Thirty-Eighth

an authentic narrative and record of the organization of the thirty-eighth regiment

of Wis. Vol. Infy, and the part taken by it in the late war

Solon W. Pierce

Battle Fields and Camp Fires of the Thirty-Eighth
an authentic narrative and record of the organization of the thirty-eighth regiment of Wis.
Vol. Infy, and the part taken by it in the late war

ISBN/EAN: 9783337255954

Printed in Europe, USA, Canada, Australia, Japan

Cover: Foto ©Andreas Hilbeck / pixelio.de

More available books at **www.hansebooks.com**

AND

CAMP FIRES

OF THE

THIRTY-EIGHTH.

AN AUTHENTIC NARRATIVE AND RECORD OF THE ORGANIZATION
OF THE THIRTY-EIGHTH REGIMENT OF WIS. VOL. INF'Y, AND
THE PART TAKEN BY IT IN THE LATE WAR, A SHORT
BIOGRAPHICAL SKETCH OF EACH COMMISSIONED
OFFICER, AND THE NAME, AGE AT TIME OF
ENLISTMENT, NATIVITY, RESIDENCE AND
OCCUPATION OF EVERY ENLISTED
MAN, WITH NOTES OF INCI-
DENTS RELATING
TO THEM.

BY LIEUT. S. W. PIERCE.

MILWAUKEE :
DAILY WISCONSIN PRINTING HOUSE.

1866.

PIERCE, S   W.

Battle fields and camp fires of the Thirty-
eighth. An authentic narrative and record of
the organization of the Thirty-eighth regiment
of Wis. vol. inf'y, and the part taken by it in
the late war, a short biographical sketch of each
commissioned officer and the name, age at time
of enlistment, nativity, residence and occupation of every enlisted man, with notes of incidents relating to them.   Milwaukee,Daily Wisconsin printing house,1866.
254p.

CONTENTS.

CHAPTER I.

CHAPTER II.

CHAPTER III.

CHAPTER IV.

PREFACE.

The task of writing the following pages was undertaken at the request of several gentlemen, holding various positions in the Thirty-Eighth Regiment, who desired that an authentic narrative of the part it had performed in the War of the Great Rebellion, toward vindicating the authority of the Government, might be given to the world. The task was not undertaken without many misgivings. It involved much patient and close attention, and even after weeks spent in collecting the material, where cannon

" Shrieked their horror, boom for boom,"

all his labors and pains-taking in the collection of data might be swept away by a single mischance of war. Added to this was the fact that he felt a great diffidence in undertaking the work, knowing how inadequate he was to the task of doing justice to as brave and noble a band of men as ever battled for the Right. However, he finally determined to make the effort, and the result is this little volume.

The author does not claim that it is entirely per-

fect. Much of the data was collected while the Regiment lay under fire in front of Petersburg. Again, when he visited Madison, as late as the middle of last September, for the purpose of correcting and verifying the "Regimental Record," he was unable to find any Muster-Out Roll of Company A on file in the Adjutant General's office, and therefore the record of that company is not as full as that of the others.

In this connection, the author would express the great obligation he is under to his brother officers, for many courtesies extended to him—especially to Gen. Bintliff, Col. Pier, who furnished the material for that portion of the work which relates to the First Battalion, and to Lieut. W. E. Maxson, many of whose letters are embodied in the work.

The map to accompany the work will be sent as soon as it can be prepared and worked off.

If this little work shall serve to keep fresh, in the memories of his comrades, the scenes through which the Thirty-Eighth passed, and enable them to occasionally spend a pleasant hour, in the quiet and peace of home, in "fighting their battles o'er," it will fulfill the greatest desire of

THE AUTHOR.

JANUARY 15TH, 1866.

CONTENTS.

CHAPTER I.

CHAPTER II.

CHAPTER III.

CHAPTER IV.

CHAPTER V.

CHAPTER VI.

CHAPTER VII.

CHAPTER VIII.

CHAPTER IX.

CHAPTER X.

CHAPTER XI.

CHAPTER XII.

CHAPTER XIII.

CHAPTER XIV.

CHAPTER XV.

CHAPTER XVI.

CHAPTER XVII.

BIOGRAPHICAL SKETCHES.

REGIMENTAL RECORD.

BATTLE FIELDS

AND

CAMP FIRES

OF THE

38th. WISCONSIN VOLUNTEERS.

CHAPTER I.

The War, with varied fortunes of successes and reverses to the National arms, had dragged its bloody length through three years. McDowell, McClellan, Burnside and Hooker had successively advanced to assault the Rebel capital, and each in his turn was driven back with disaster. Antietam only saved the North from invasion; and the victory of Gettysburg only compelled the insurgents to retire within their own lines. Nowhere in all the Eastern States, in rebellion, had we made progress at all commensurate with the expectations of the loyal people of the North.

In the West, our arms had met with gratifying success. Sweeping from the North along the Mississippi, the invincible army of Grant had surmounted all obstacles and captured Vicksburg. New Orleans

B

had fallen an easy conquest into our hands. Banks
had succeeded in clearing all the lower Mississippi,
and five days after the capitulation of Vicksburg,
received the surrender of Port Hudson, the last
Rebel stronghold on the great "Father of Waters."
Kentucky and Missouri were firmly established in
the Union, and the greater part of Tennessee was
recovered and remained in possession of the National arms, while, at the same time, we had secured and
retained important positions in Georgia and other
portions of the rebellious States. The Mississippi
was open to navigation from Cairo to the Gulf, and
the rebellion practically cut in twain.

Notwithstanding these successes, however, on the
part of the Union armies in the Southwest, the rebels
were still as arrogant and defiant as ever, and it was
evident, during all the winter of 1863–4, that the
national forces must be largely augmented in order
to bring the contest to a speedy and successful
issue.

The successive calls of the President, for men to
fill up our armies, had been promptly responded to
on the part of Wisconsin, until the spring of 1864.
Owing to a variety of causes, recruiting had been
very dull through the latter part of the winter, and
it was a source of pride and gratification to the people of our State, when it was announced that our
quota was full. But our self gratulation was of
short duration, for, hardly was the announcement
made, before the telegraph flashed over the country
the call of the President of April 3d, for 200,000 men,
and the further ungratifying news that the large boun-

ties heretofore paid by the Government, would immediately cease.

These heavy calls for men were severely felt by the sparse population of the Northwest—and the unscrupulous opponents of the war, seized the opportunity to fan every latent spark of discontent into a flame of intense dissatisfaction. Everything that a perverse ingenuity could invent to throw obstacles in the way of a successful prosecution of the war was resorted to. The President was declared to be a brutal, perjured tyrant, who only waged war for the purpose of immolating its victims upon the altar of his bloody ambition, and that he might trample the liberties of our people under his feet. Gen. Grant, to whom had been assigned the chief command of the Union armies, was simply a butcher, delighting in the effusion of blood, but possessed of no military abilities of any merit whatever. The war was declared to be "Lincoln's war," and the brave men who had gone forth to battle for the salvation of the national existence were stigmatized as "Lincoln's hirelings."

In this trying hour, the executive of our State, true to the interests of the nation and the honor of Wisconsin, issued a call, earnestly urging the people to furnish the number of men required by the quota of our State. The organization of two more regiments—the 37th and 38th—were at once undertaken. Camp Randall, Madison, Wis., was designated as the place to rendezvous. Recruiting commissions were liberally issued, and the work of raising the required number of men earnestly began.

Early in April, nearly five companies of the men raised for the Thirty-Eighth had assembled at Madison. On the 15th of that month, four companies, A, B, C, and D, were mustered into the military service of the United States. The companies were respectively placed under the commands of Captains Charles T. Carpenter, R. N. Roberts, S. D. Woodworth, and James Woodford. From the time of being mustered into service until leaving for the seat of war, these companies remained in Camp Randall, drilling and otherwise preparing for the work before them. May 3d was the day appointed for the battalion to leave Madison, and proceed to Annapolis, Md., at which place it was to report. The battalion was commanded by Lieut. Col. Pier and Major Larkin.

In the morning, previous to starting, the battalion was drawn up in line of battle, to witness the pleasing spectacle of the presentation of an elegant sword, sash and belt by the battalion to Col. Bintliff. The ceremonies were very appropriate and interesting. The presentation was made, on behalf of the battalion, by Lieut. Col. Pier, in a neat and effective speech, which was responded to by Col. Bintliff in a feeling and happy manner. Immediately after the ceremonies of the presentation were over, the battalion embarked on the cars, and bidding a soldier's "good-bye" to those who were to join them in the field when the balance of the regiment should be raised, started on its way to "Dixie."

While marching from camp to the cars, the battalion passed the 30th Wisconsin, under Colonel Haskell, which was drilling on the parade grounds. The

Colonel brought that regiment into line, and saluted the 38th with three parting cheers, which were heartily responded to by the latter. Little did either party then think that their next meeting would be on the hotly contested field at Cold Harbor, the 36th torn and bloody with its leader slain, and the Thirty-Eighth, burning with high hopes, about to receive its first baptism of battle.

CHAPTER II.

The manager of the Soldiers Rest at Chicago having been previously notified by telegraph of the movement of the battalion, the agents of the Institution met it on its arrival in that city and conducted it to the "Rest." Willing hands and pleasant smiles waited upon the "boys in blue" and spread before them a bountiful repast. The hour was enlivened by music and song, and all "went merry as a marriage bell," until the shrill whistle of the locomotive called the battalion aboard the train for Pittsburg.

The memories of the pleasant hour spent at the Soldiers' Rest in Chicago, will live forever in the hearts of those present.

The soldierly appearance, and gentlemanly conduct of the men elicited universal praise from all, and the several newspapers of the city spoke of them in the most flattering manner. Arriving at Pittsburg early in the morning of the 5th, the battalion was welcomed by the agents of the Soldier's Rest and received the hospitalities of Pittsburg.

To the excellent and abundant meal spread before them the men did ample justice.

Here the managers of the Pennsylvania Central Railroad proposed to transport the battalion over their road in box cars. The utmost care had been

exercised, thus far, to prevent injury to the cars used,
and knowing that there were plenty of passenger
coaches, the Railroad Superintendent was politely
informed that the battalion would remain in Pittsburg until suitable cars were furnished for its transportation. In less than an hour the troops were all
seated in elegant coaches and moving toward Baltimore. Upon reporting the following day, Lieut.
Col. Pier found the Ninth Army Corps had left.
Here the men first tasted the realities of a soldier's
life. Crowded into a close, dark basement, they were
there kept under guard until they left the city.
However, the battalion was ordered to report immediately to Washington, at which place it arrived
about midnight on the 6th, and was comfortably
accomodated at the Soldiers' Rest near the Railroad
depot. Sunday, May 8th, it was moved across Long
Bridge, and encamped on Arlington Heights.
Here it was furnished with a full supply of Camp and
Garrison equipage, a camp was laid out, and the usual
daily routine of drill and camp life commenced.
Officers and men improved rapidly and were attaining
to a fine state of discipline. The unavoidable ailings
and minor diseases, such as colds, measles, mumps,
etc., always more or less attendant on the change from
civil to military life, were borne with commendable
fortitude by the men and finally overcome. Under
such circumstances it was earnestly hoped the battalion might remain there in camp until it should be
joined by the balance of the Regiment.

These hopes, however, were fated to disappointment, for orders were received for the battalion to
move, on the 30th of May, to Alexandria, and there

embark. Promptly at sunrise, with knapsacks and haversacks packed, the men were in line. Lt. Col. Pier then briefly addressed them; told them they were about to move into unseen and unknown dangers; that they would be called upon to undergo privations, hardships and exposure that would severely tax their patience and endurance; that he should trust to their courage, patriotism and manliness to supply any deficiency of discipline that the limited time allotted them for instructions had prevented their attaining; and that, whether on the march or in the battle-field, he should expect every man to guard, maintain and defend to the last, the reputation of the regiment, the fair name of our State, and the principles for which they fought.

Nothing could exceed the enthusiastic readiness of the officers and men to enter on the campaign then opening for them. The march to Alexandria was extremely pleasant and interesting. Avoiding the dusty highway, conducted by its trusty guide, "Charley," the battalion followed green by-paths across fields, through forests and grassy lanes, over gurgling brooks, keeping step to the stirring measures of martial music. A battalion of the 1st Minnesota regiment accompanied it on its march, and arrived at the same time at Alexandria; but aside from these, of all the troops that started from Arlington Heights at the same time, none arrived until later in the day. Having arrived first, the officers in charge gave Lieut. Col. Pier the choice of the boats there assembled for the transportation of troops. The steamer Emilie was selected, and the Thirty-

Eighth and the battalion of the 1st Minnesota immediately embarked.

The voyage down the Potomac River, through the
Chesapeake Bay, up the York and Pamunky Rivers,
was very pleasant, and was enjoyed by all.

CHAPTER III.

The battalion arrived at White House Landing at noon, on the 1st day of June, and immediately reported to Gen. Ames, and was ordered to disembark and encamp. There was no land transportation to be had, and all the material, baggage and stores of the regiment had to be carried by the men more than a mile.

The battalion was assigned to the Provisional Brigade, commanded by Col. Johnson.

On June 3d, the regimental commanders of the brigade were ordered to break camp, and report immediately at headquarters with their commands. A new position was to be taken, and the regiment that should report first, it was understood, would be assigned the post of honor, the right of the brigade. The race was a spirited one; the Thirty-Eighth, leading the van, was first in and won the position.

In the new position taken by the brigade, slight earthworks were thrown up. Here, too, the 1st Minnesota battalion was temporarily consolidated with that of the Thirty-Eighth.

On the following Sunday, the regiment marched to Cold Harbor, a distance of eleven miles, as escort for a wagon train. It arrived at that place in the evening, and bivouaced for the night. Next day it

returned to the White House. While at Cold Harbor a heavy and continuous musketry fire broke out along the lines. For the first time the men heard the roar and thunder of battle.

On the 9th, the battalion again escorted a wagon train to the front. The rainy weather had rendered the roads almost impassable. All night the men struggled and floundered along as best they could. The train was nearly two miles in length, and when one wagon mired or became disabled, or an exhausted mule fell down, or any impediment occurred sufficient to stop one wagon, it would stop all behind it. It was thus rendered necessary for the men to take hold and build bridges, raise sunken wagons, unharness dead and dying mules, and perform many other laborious acts. Thus they alternately marched and halted, until 2 o'clock A. M., when they arrived at their destination.

Then the men lay down to rest their overtasked energies. But such a rest! Scattered thickly over the ground were scores of dead horses and mules, whose decaying carcasses emitted a noisome stench that was oppressive and sickening in the extreme. The result was that many of the men vomited up their suppers, and scarcely any were able to eat their accustomed breakfast.

That day the battalion reported to Gen. Meade, commanding the army of the Potomac, and was by him assigned to the Ninth corps. The Minnesota battalion was assigned to the Second corps. Upon reporting to Gen. Burnside, commanding the Ninth corps, the battalion was finally assigned to the Third brigade of the First division. The latter command-

ed by Gen. Ledlie, and the former by Col. Johnson.

Next to the 30th of July, the day Gen. Burnside's
mine was exploded, the 10th of June may be ranked
for the intense heat of the sun. Not a breath of
wind stirring, and the dust, notwithstanding the
rain of the day before, was fully a foot deep, and
being disturbed by thousands of horses, mules and
wagons, rendered marching almost insufferable.
The battalion was so gray with dust that it might
have been readily mistaken for rebels.

The next day it constructed its first line of breastworks, and although, during the successive months
the regiment built many miles of field fortifications,
and learned to build them quicker, it never erected
more perfect ones than those at Cold Harbor.

During the afternoon the battalion was detailed
to perform its first picket duty. The same day it
was also, by special orders, transferred to the Third
division, commanded by Gen. O. B. Willcox, and by
that officer assigned to the 1st Brigade, commanded
by Col. (afterward General) J. F. Hartranft. Relieved from picket duty at midnight, it marched to the
new position assigned it, occupying a line of rifle-
pits from which the enemy had recently been driven,
and which was still swept by his fire. Here the battalion lay, and amid the thunder of bursting shells,
and the whizzing of bullets, learned its lesson, pre-
paratory to more active operations in the field with
the army of the Potomac.

It was while laying here, June 12th, that the Regiment met its first loss. Corporal Hackley Adams,
of company A, was on the picket line, and with seve-

ral others was watching a troublesome rebel sharp-shooter, who was posted in a tree a few hundred yards in front.

One of the men with Adams, Franklin Parks of company D, was mortally wounded by a shot from the rebel, and fell exposed to full view, and in easy range of his deadly rifle. Regardless of personal safety, Hackley generously sprang to the assistance of his wounded comrade and removed him to a place of comparative safety. There, although himself still exposed, he continued to minister to the wounded man, and while so doing, fell, pierced with a bullet from the same gun by which the other was wounded. The dead and dying were immediately carried to the rear, a rude coffin was constructed, and a sorrowing company followed the remains of their brave and noble comrade to his final resting place.

A mild, quiet, unassuming boy was Hackley. None stood higher in the estimation of the battalion; none were more attentive, dutiful, or soldierly in their conduct than he.

Parks died about an hour after him who had so nobly lost his life in ministering to his needs, and was buried, as he deserved to be, with a soldier's honors, by the members of his company. Orders were received that day to be prepared to move at early dusk. At the designated time the column moved to the rear. Night and day, stopping only occasionally to take a hasty cup of coffee, across fields, along by-roads and highways, over hills, through forests, rivers and marshes, the men, with heavy loads, tracked the weary journey.

Wagons broke down—horses, tired out or disa-

bled, were shot on the spot—yet the men still moved forward, eating and drinking as chance offered an opportunity, and sleeping as they walked. Thus passed four days and nights, when Gen. Burnside received information that if he could arrive at Petersburg soon enough, that city, as well as Richmond, would inevitably fall. The news was read to the troops. Weary, lame, footsore and exhausted by hardship and exposure as the troops were, the ranks were at once closed up, and the column moved off in quick time, while loud hurrahs bespoke the indomitable spirit that pervaded the hearts of all.

CHAPTER IV.

On the evening of the 16th of June, having crossed the James River near City Point, the battalion arrived in front of Petersburg. The heavy boom of artillery and the sharp rattle of musketry told but too surely that the battle had already begun. It seemed hardly possible that these men, so fatigued and exhausted, could be expected to take part in the battle; yet the movements indicated that they were to do so. Lines of battle extending for miles, were formed, a hasty supper eaten, and the advance commenced.

Shot, shell, grape and cannister screeched and screamed through the air. Darkness came, and still the battle raged on. About nine o'clock Lieut. Col. Pier was ordered to take possession of an earthwork from which the enemy had just been driven, and to hold his command in readiness to support the line of battle then moving forward. The command was immediately moved to its assigned position. Here the gallant battalion, completely worn out, standing at an "order arms," and leaning against the earthworks, while the terrible conflict raged but a few rods in front, and artillery thundered and musketry rattled, slept the sleep of exhaustion.

Thus the night passed. Thousands had fallen du-

c

ring the fight. The dead and wounded scattered over the field and carried by scores to the rear, told how fierce and desperate had been the struggle. Still the enemy held his ground, and it was decided that the Ninth Corps must measure strength with him.

The order came at nine o'clock in the morning.

The lines were formed, the first brigade in front, the Thirty-Eighth on the right of the brigade. For two hours, and while the troops were moving into position, the battalion lay exposed to a severe artillery fire from the enemy's forts and batteries. The final dispositions were at length made, and at 12 o'clock, noon, the order came to move forward. The entire line charged at once. The course of the Thirty-Eighth lay through a field in which the corn was about knee high. A thick cloud of smoke and dust soon covered the field, and hid everything, beyond a few paces, from sight. For twenty minutes the men stood up against the hot, deadly stream of fire from the enemy's works, but a mistake of the engineer officer as to the direction of the rebel lines, caused the assault to fail.

But not until the Thirty-Eighth had struck the enemy's works, and its wounded and dead were falling inside of his lines, was it discovered that the other portions of our line were falling back in disorder, and that the day was lost. Then with a quick "right-about" the Thirty-Eighth gave up the fight, and relinquished the ground it had so gallantly won, and in comparatively good order fell back to the ravine in which the lines were originally formed. It was during this charge that Major Larkin while

gallantly leading the men, sword and hat in hand, fell, severely wounded, the ball entering his right side, just above the hip. In the smoke and dust the fall of the Major was unoticed, and his absence not observed until the line had been reformed, when it was learned that he had been wounded and left upon the field. A wounded officer who had managed to crawl off the field, gave the information that the Major lay about half way to the enemy's lines, under a severe fire from both sides.

Several officers immediately started to his rescue, and Capt. Carpenter, springing forward to where he lay, succeeded in bringing him off the field.

The lines were again aligned, and everything being ready, the troops at seven o'clock, P. M., again moved forward to the assault. But, during the intervening time the enemy had not been idle, and the fire under which our men now moved forward, was, if possible, even more severe and terrible than that they met during the first assault. This move, however, was destined to be far more successful than the former one. The enemy was driven from his works, and compelled to fall back upon the line of the Petersburg and Norfolk railroad, and the national forces, weary with the heavy fighting, rested until morning.

The next day, the 18th, towards evening, our forces, including the Thirth-Eighth, charged and captured the enemy's works along the railroad. Then, every man that could be, was set to work on fortifications. Breast-works, forts, covered ways, and rifle-pits sprung into existence as if by magic. The loss of the battalion in the two days—17th and 18th of June

—was three killed and thirty-six wounded,—six of
them, mortally, and four missing. Among the
wounded were Lt. Col. Pier, Maj. Larkin, Capt. Carpenter, and Lieutenants Hayward and Wright. All,
however, were able to, and remained upon the field
with their respective commands, except Maj. Larkin,
whose wound, considered mortal at the time, was so
severe as to render him unable to stand upon his
feet.

Early dawn of the 19th of June saw two opposing
lines of earthworks, consisting of forts, batteries and
breastworks, almost within a stone's throw of each
other. From either side, during the day, a sharp
continuous volley of musketry flashed forth.

A stream of dead, dying and wounded, was constantly passing to the rear. During the day the men
were requried to keep constantly at their posts with
guns in their hands. As soon as darkness would hide
their forms from the enemy, they were obliged to take
the pick and shovel and work at strengthening the
defenses. Never did troops perform more arduous
duties. Exposed to unimaginable hardships—doing
fatigue duty of every nature, for eighteen consecutive
days these heroes fought by day and shoveled by
night. They went to the spring for water at the peril
of their lives. They rested a moment that tired nature
might recuperate, but rested exposed to shot and
shell and every missile of death. Nature could not
always bear this terrible strain. The strongest and
most robust must yield in time to overwork beneath
a hot and sultry sun, irregular meals, or rather no
meals, broken sleep and uncleansed clothes and body.
So, gradually the sick list increased and the number

" present for duty " grew less and less. What was true of the Thirty-Eighth was equally true of the whole army.

July fourth, what was left of the battalion was relieved, and moved out of the pits, to the rear about three quarters of a mile, where a camp was formed and the men rested. But nature could not quickly recover her exhausted energies beneath the sultry rays of a southern summer's sun, under fire and the excitement caused by being so near the lines. Rest and good nursing were needed, and these could not be obtained in the field during the exigencies of an active campaign. But the relief from the immediate front gave the men an opportunity to wash and cleanse their persons and clothing, and to obtain and cook their rations with much greater regularity. Notwithstanding these more favorable conditions, the men were so worn and diseased by exposure and overwork, and perhaps somewhat discouraged, the number of sick continued to increase until on Sunday, July 17th, only twenty men and six officers were reported for duty, and these were ordered into the pits again to assist in repelling an expected attack by the enemy.

The stream of fire from either line continued, with unabated intensity, night and day. From 4,000 to 11,000 rounds of ammunition were expended daily by each regiment. Every hour some were killed or wounded. For weeks the opposing forces watched each other through their respective loop and port holes, and sent a bullet whizzing at every indication of life that exposed itself in the enemy's lines. Men had learned to keep well under the cover of the earthworks, and to dread any exposure to the uner-

ring and deadly aim of the enemy's sharpshooters. On the 26th of July, the battalion was joined by company E, commanded by Capt. Newton S. Ferris, a decided acquisition to the effective force of the battalion.

CHAPTER V.

The morning of the ever memorable 30th of July, broke over the besiegers and the besieged. Companies B and E, occupied a position in the most advanced line of works, while the remainder of the battalion was posted in the second line, a few rods to the rear. At early dawn the men made their accustomed preparations, expecting to be relieved in a few moments, and to move to the rear to procure the rest so much needed by every soldier, who after being under fire all day is obliged to keep watch during the night.

It was, while waiting the expected relief, that the battalion was surprised to behold and hear the terrible explosion of Burnside's mine, under the rebel fort directly in our front and only a few rods distant. The following extract from the columns of the New York *Times*, written by an eye-witness, gives a very graphic account of the position and the reasons for the movement:

"Headquarters in front of Army of Potomac,
Saturday Evening, July 30th, 1864.

With the passage of the James was exhausted all possibilities of a movement by the left flank, with Richmond as the objective point. Nothing, therefore, remained to Gen. Grant but to assault the rebel

lines in front of him at Petersburg. The past six
weeks have been devoted to preparation for this assault. From day to day, by the aid of the shovel
and the pick, our lines have been insidiously advanced by zigzag and covered ways, until the out-
lying pickets of both armies have scarcely averaged
five hundred yards distance between them. Along
portions of the line, the interval between the rifle-
pits was scarcely one hundred and fifty yards. The
ground over which our advances have been made is
itself a series of natural fortifications, adding vastly
to the difficulty of taking possession of it. Perhaps
your readers will form a more perfect opinion of its
features, if I tell them that it very much resembles
Greenwood cemetery in its profile.

There were similar hills and eminences, sloping
more or less precipitately into ravines, which inter-
sect at every conceivable angle, and many of the
elevations are thickly wooded. Over ground of this
impracticable nature, our men have sturdily fought
and dug their way, driving the enemy before them,
until only one hill remained for them to take, to place
our guns in a position commanding, at easy range,
the town of Petersburg. It is known as Cemetery
Hill. Its crest, frowning with guns, is not more than
800 yards distant from our advanced works, and its
gently sloping sides are welted with long rows of
earthworks, pitted with redoubts and redans, and
ridged with serried salients and curtains, and all the
skillful defences known to able military engineers.

The vital importance, to us, of this point, will
readily be admitted. To gain it by direct assault
must necessarily cost many lives; but to gain it in

the cheapest manner, gave occasion for that high
strategy of which Gen. Grant has long since proved
himself the master. Therefore it was, that on Tuesday night last, the Second Corps, under Gen. Han-
cock, and two divisions of cavalry, under Gen. Sheridan, and another division under Gen. Kautz, crossed
the James River for the purpose of engaging the
enemy, who, misled by some preliminary operations
of Gen. Foster's command at Deep Bottom, and of a
portion of the Nineteenth Corps at Strawberry
Plains, a mile below, had, a day or two earlier, reinforced the troops in the vicinity of Malvern Hill.
The demonstration here had precisely the effect
which Gen. Grant desired. Fearing a serious attack, Lee dispatched a column, estimated at from
12,000 to 15,000 strong, from before Petersburg, and
the railroad between Petersburg and Richmond was
kept busy on Friday and Friday night in transport-
ing the troops. To keep up the rebel General's de-
lusion, an immense train of more than 400 empty
covered wagons, mainly the transportation of the
Sixth Corps, crossed the Appomattox on Friday, in
broad daylight, in full view of the rebel signal look-
outs at Bermuda Hundred, as if destined for the
army at Deep Bottom. But on Friday night, as the
rebels were hurriedly taking possession of their new
line, the Second Corps and the cavalry were quietly
withdrawn, with an additional facility for rapid
movement in a third pontoon bridge, laid across the
James in the afternoon.

By daylight this morning these troops were nearly
all in position to co-operate with the remainder of
the army in the attack. The strategy was, there-

fore, perfect, and no share of the reverse can be
attributed to failure in this part of the programme.

All these stratagems, too, were conducted with
such secrecy, that information of their precise bearing
was narrowed down to the circle of the corps commanders. Until late on Friday night, few persons
in the army were disposed to believe differently from
what Gen. Lee suspected, viz: that a movement upon Richmond was intended, from the north side of
the James, and were only undeceived when, at one
o'clock this morning, the troops were got into position for the assault. The tactics of the movement
were under Gen. Meade's direction. His arrangement of troops and order of battle was as follows:
The Eighteenth Corps (Gen. Ord) was withdrawn
on Thursday morning from its position on the extreme right, resting on the Appomattox, (being relieved by Mott's division of the Second Corps,) and
massed in the rear of the Ninth Corps (Burnside's),
the centre of our line, in front of which the attack
was to be initiated. The extreme left, held by the
Fifth Corps (Warren's), was to be in readiness to
advance as soon as Burnside pierced the works in
front of him.

Collaterally, but in unison with the advance of the
infantry, every piece of siege artillery posted along
the line was ordered to open simultaneously upon
the enemy at a given signal, made by the explosion
of a mine containing eight tons of powder, which was
placed directly beneath the rebel battery which
Burnside was to assault. Not only were the siege
pieces to open a fierce fire, but all the field artillery
which could be got into position after the opening of

the battle, was to advance as opportunity offered, and bring their batteries into play. Upon this awful fire of heavy guns, it was natural that great stress should be placed, in the expectation that the shock of its suddenness would have a demoralizing effect, and so make the way of the infantry easier. So far all was well arranged; success was promising, and much confidence was felt in the result.

The time fixed for the assault was 3½ o'clock, when, without any moon, an almost Cimmerian darkness would effectually shut out from the enemy the unavoidable stir and bustle of the troops as they got into position. But just here the first misfortune of the day occurred. Upon attempting to fire the mine, the fuse or slow match failed, and another was tried, with a similar result. The third was succesful in its mission, but the hour's delay had made it broad daylight, and, in consequence, the enemy's suspicions were aroused, (at least along a portion of his front,) and we were robbed of the advantage of a suprise.

This was a very great misfortune. The army felt it to be such as they stood in suspense and silent impatience in the cold gray of the morning, crouching on their arms. Of the effect of the explosion you have already been apprised. The mine had been talked of in the army for weeks, but only talked of with bated breath, although whisperings concerning it had been wafted over from the rebels. Clearly they did not know its precise locality, and few on our side I suspect, were any wiser. It has been tacitly acknowledged as an improper subject for conversation, and the most curious have appeared to feel the propriety of checking themselves.

The noise of the explosion was a dull, rumbling thud, preceded, I am told, by a few second's swaying and quaking of the ground in the immediate . vicinity. The earth was rent along the entire course of the excavation, heaving slowly and majestically to the surface, and folding sideways to exhibit a deep and yawning chasm, comparable, as much as anything else, to a river gorged with ice, and breaking up under the influence of a freshet. But there was a grander effect than this observable also. Where the charge in the burrow was heaviest, directly under the rebel work, an immense mass of dull red earth was thrown high in air, in three broad columns, diverging from a single base, and, to my mind, assuming the shape of a Prince of Wales' feather, of collossal proportions. Those near the spot say that clods of earth weighing near a ton, and cannon, and human forms, and gun-carriages, and small arms, were all distinctly seen shooting upward in that fountain of horror, and fell again in shapeless and pulverized atoms. The explosion fully accomplished what was intended. It demolished the six-gun battery and its garrison of one regiment of South Carolina troops, and acted as the wedge which opened the way to the assault. Our men were to rush through this breach, and so beyond upon the second line of works which crown the crest of Cemetery Hill, thus compelling the enemy to evacuate the first line, or, what was more probable, to surrender under the fire of our artillery.

The awful instant of the explosion had scarcely passed when the dull morning air was made stagnant by the thunder of our artillery. From ninety-

five pieces, niched in every hill side commanding the enemy's position, there belched out sheets of flame and milk-white smoke, while the shot and shell sped forward, screeching, howling, rumbling, like the rushing of a hundred railroad trains. But why attempt to give an idea of such indescribable sound? The sudden transition from utter silence to fiercest clamor was terrible. So the rude combat raged without sign of slackening for two long hours. At first the enemy was slow in replying to our fire, but gradually their lines were brought into action, and in less than half an hour banks of angry smoke partially veiled the scene from both sides.

In accordance with the plan of battle the First Division of the Ninth Corps, (Ledlie's,) was made the assaulting column. Gen. Ledlie formed his troops in three lines of battle, having each a front of about six hundred. The Second Brigade of this Division, (Col. Marshall,) led the assault, followed by the First Brigade, (Gen. W. F. Bartlett), and the third line made up of the Third Brigade (Col. Gould's.) The left of Ledlie's division was supported by Brig. Gen. Hartranft's Brigade of the Third Division, (Willcox's) and its right by Gen. Griffin's Brigade of Potter's Division. The Fourth Division of the Ninth Corps, (all negroes,) was posted directly in the rear of the assaulting column, to press forward whenever practicable. The Fourteenth New York Heavy Artillery were the first to enter the breach made by the explosion. They bounded forward at the word, in the midst of the shock of the artillery, through the dense clouds of flying dust, and clambering over the debris, found themselves violently pushed down into the

yawning crater. The sight which there met them
must have been appalling. Bodies of dead rebels
crushed and mangled out of all resemblance to humanity, writhing forms partly buried, arms protru-
ding here and legs struggling there—a very hell of
horror and torture, confined to a space fifty feet in
length and half as many wide. But the time was
not favorable to the play of human promptings.
This chaos of mangled humanity mixed with debris
of implements and munitions of war must be un-
heeded. Enough for the storming party to do was
found in exhuming two pieces of rebel cannon with
their caissons, and, in obedience to the law of self-
preservation, turning these guns upon the enemy, who
was throwing into the crater a shower of shells and
minnie balls from the hill beyond, and from points
on either side, which they still held on the first line.
Getting these pieces into position promptly, and under cover of their fire, the assaulting column was
reformed, and at the word of command dashed forward once more to storm the crest of the hill. It
was a task too great. They gallantly essayed it,
and nearly gained the summit, subjected all the
time to a withering fire, which increased in fierce-
ness at every step, until they became the center of
a converging storm of shot and shell. Attacked on
the right flank and the left flank, in front and rear,
they were compelled to fall back to the partial protection of the crater, leaving their course thickly
strewn with the dying and the dead.

The colored troops, upon the heel of this repulse,
were ordered to charge, and they moved out gallantly. A hundred yards gained and they wavered. Then

the Thirty-ninth Maryland regiment, which led, became panic-stricken and broke through to the rear, spreading demoralization swiftly. Their officers urged them, entreated them, threatened them, but failed to rally them, and, the mass, broken and shattered, swept back like a torrent into the crater that was literally choked with white troops. The confusion, incident to this wholesale crowding and crushing of the negro soldiers into the ranks of the white troops, very nearly caused the panic to spread. Had such been the result, it might have been fortunate, and many a brave fellow who afterwards fell, might have escaped his fate. But at the moment the rebel fire, which had been murderously directed on the place, materially slackened, and the white soldiers recovered their stamina. Our lines were once more straightened, and just in time to check an impetuous charge, which was afterwards repeated, and with a similar result of heavy loss to the assailants.

So the morning waned. It became apparent, doubtless, that the position gained could not be held without more sacrifice of life than could be well afforded at this time.

At any rate, this seems a fair inference, or the other corps would have been ordered to advance upon those portions of the first line still held by the enemy, and as far as I can ascertain, no such order was given. On the contrary, about noon the order was given to retire—a matter not easy of execution, as to gain our works an open space must be traversed, over which one man in every twenty was sure to be brought down by the cross-fire that swept the spot."

A correspondent of the New York *World*, writing next day from the scene of action, gives the following:

"After the explosion, at an early hour yesterday morning, everything betokened a brilliant victory; but soon after matters assumed a different aspect, a part of the attacking force having given way, exposing the balance to an enfilading fire from both artillery and infantry.

The programme was as follows: The mine to be exploded at 3 A. M.; the batteries to open at once along the entire line, immediately after the explosion, and the 9th Corps to make the charge, supported by the 18th Corps, Ayers' division of the 5th Corps, and the 3d division of the 2d Corps.

The greater part of the arrangement was carried out as ordered, although the commencement was later than the hour designated, on account of the fuse going out twice. The explosion took place at precisely 40 minutes past 4 o'clock. The roar of artillery that followed was almost deafening.

At 5 o'clock the charge was made, and the fort, with a part of the line on each side, was carried in a most brilliant manner. The 2d division, which was in the center, advanced and carried the second line, a short distance beyond the fort, and rested, holding their ground with the utmost determination. At this time the colored division, under Gen. Julius White, was pushed forward and ordered to charge and carry the crest of the hill, which would have decided the contest. The troops advanced in good order as far as the first line, where they received a galling fire, which checked them; and although quite a

number kept advancing, the greater portion seemed to become utterly demoralized, part of them taking refuge in the fort, and the balance running to the rear as fast as possible.

They were rallied and again pushed forward, but without success. The greater part of their officers being killed or wounded during this time, they seemed to be without any one to manage them, and finally fell back to the rear, out of the range of the volleys of canister and musketry that were ploughing through the ranks."

It was through this storm of every conceivable missile, that companies B and E of the Thirty-Eighth charged toward the enemy's works—going forward until ordered to halt, and retreating only when commanded to do so. The other companies, though not taking part in the charge, were under fire, and all suffered more or less.

At 3 o'clock P. M. the gallant Ninth Corps, having performed untold prodigies of heroism, and failing only because it was not properly supported—or rather not supported at all—with torn and shattered ranks, was driven back to our lines, after having lost four thousand men.

In the Thirty-Eighth, of the officers who took part in the assault, Lieut. Ballard was the only one who escaped unharmed. Capt. Ferris, of company E, was killed, and Lieut. Holton wounded. The loss of the battalion was 7 killed, 16 wounded, and 10 prisoners and missing.

Darkness, gloom and despondency now gathered around, and spread its pall over the national camp.

The lack of sympathy, unity of council, and con-

D

cert of action among the leaders, as evidenced by
the almost entire neglect to render any support to
the Ninth Corps during the terrible hours of the 30th
of July, only served to increase and intensify these
feelings, so naturally following the heels of defeat
and disaster.   Officers and men alike felt its benumbing influence.

The usual firing and constant duty in the pits and
trenches was again resumed.   Day after day the
men lay crouching behind their works, boiling and
scorching beneath the intense rays of a southern
August sun, and suffering as only soldiers can suffer.

CHAPTER VI

August had more than half worn away. On the 19th orders came to get in readiness to move without delay. At 3 o'clock A. M. the battalion moved toward the left, in the direction of the Weldon Railroad. It rained during the previous night, and the morning was showery. Thousands of feet worked the 'earth and water into "Virginia mud." Through this the column pressed on until noon, when the battalion was halted, during a heavy shower, stacked arms, and the men proceeded to prepare such a dinner as is usual to soldiers on the march. While kindling little fires to boil their coffee, freshening their salt mackerel, or wringing the water from their saturated clothes, they were startled by the sharp rattle of musketry breaking forth from two skirmish lines, engaging each other but a short distant behind them. Instantly the men fell into line, and in four minutes the battalion was advancing in line of battle to support our skirmishers. Through ravines, ditches and brushwood it moved in fine style, keeping the files well dressed. Already the men comprehended the situation; for the first time they were to meet the enemy on open ground and equal terms. As the battalion gained a piece of open ground, the skirmish line was discovered rapidly falling back,

and the enemy closely pressing forward after it.
With a ringing "hurrah," the battalion charged forward upon the enemy. The Thirty-Seventh and
Thirty-Eighth, in the movement, became detached
from the rest of the brigade, and, passing over the
retreating skirmish line, threw themselves upon the
enemy, scattering his line in confusion. It was here,
while our forces were securing prisoners, that one of
those mistakes occurred, which, it seems, no amount
of foresight can always avoid, but which are none
the less to be regretted because they cannot be prevented. These two regiments had advanced so far
that they were mistaken, by those in the rear, for
the enemy, and our own artillery opened upon them,
making the position they held untenable, and both
regiments fell back out of range.

During the remainder of the day the enemy attacked successively upon the right, left and centre of
the national lines, but each time was driven back
with heavy loss. The successes of our arms had a
most happy effect, and never were soldiers in better
spirits than were ours upon the evening of that day.

The next day was spent by both armies in maneu-
vering for position. On the morning of the 21st, the
brigade was moved to the left and thrown across
the Weldon Railroad, the Thirty-Eighth taking a
position directly across the track. Immediately every
available man was put to work to fortify the position
occupied, for it was understood, generally, that the
day would decide the question as to which party should
hold the road. But while the Union forces were thus
busily engaged in strengthening their position, the
enemy was by no means idle; nor did he intend to

abandon the lost ground without a struggle for its recovery. Massing his forces on the front, and right and left flanks, he moved to the assault.

By ten o'clock the battle commenced. The enemy was seen emerging from the woods. In three lines of battle, at a double-quick, they bore down upon the Union lines. How little did they realize the terrible trap into the very jaws of which they were blindly rushing! Still, on they came, with battle-flags streaming and steel glistening in the morning sun.

Nearly half the open space intervening was passed over, and yet all remained quiet within the Union lines. Suddenly a hundred cannon belched forth a tornado of destruction through the rebel ranks.

Volley after volley, in rapid succession, sweep through the advancing ranks. Whole companies and regiments melt and disappear, until torn, broken, shattered, and disorganized, the mingled mass turn and flee, in wild terror, for the cover of the woods from which, only a few moments before, they had emerged confident of victory. Wild, exultant cheers rent the air, and glad hurrahs rang along the Union lines. The enemy had been met in fair fight and driven back. Then followed the stillness and quiet that always succeeds the tumult and roar of battle. For an hour all seemed quiet. Suddenly heavy firing was heard on the extreme right. The roar and tumult increased. Staff officers and orderlies rode furiously from brigade to brigade. In a moment the troops were moving at a double-quick to the *left*. What could this mean? this apparent retreat from the field of battle? Soon the movement developed itself, for troops were also seen moving from the left toward the center. The troops were being massed there

for some purpose. Gradually the firing on the wings died away; the attack on the right was only a feint to mislead us; but Gen. Grant is on the field in person, and his clear intellect has at once penetrated the enemy's movement and divined where the next blow is destined to fall.

Hardly are the troops placed in position, when another rebel column is seen advancing to assault the center. This time they come on the full run and charge directly for the railroad. Rebel batteries' open upon our line with solid shot, grape, and schrapnel. Suddenly our lines became a livid sheet of flame. Artillery and musketry swept the rebel ranks and mowed them with destructive fury. But with an indomitable bravery, worthy of a better and holier cause, the rebel column swept on. No troops, however, could long withstand the terrible fire con_centrated upon the rebel column. It faltered, wavered, swayed, and then broke and fled in wild confusion. Many threw down their arms, and, with uplifted hands, made for our lines, preferring to surrender as prisoners of war, rather than run the hazard of an attempt to leave the field. As soon as it was discovered that the enemy had faltered, a line of battle sprang forward over our temporary works, and with shouts of victory pursued the fleeing enemy.

> " The fight was o'er: the flashing through the gloom,
> Which robes the cannon as he wings a tomb,
> Had ceased; and sulphury vapors upward driven
> Had left the earth, and but polluted heaven:
> The rattling roar which rung in every volley
> Had left the valleys to their melancholy;
> No more they shrieked their horror, boom for boom;
> The strife was done, the vanquished had their doom."
>
> *—The Island: Canto III.*

Thus were fought and won the successive battles that wrested forever from the confederacy the Weldon railroad, one of its chiefest and most important lines of communication and supply to the forces it had gathered for the defence of the rebel capital. He struggled terribly before it was wrenched from his grasp, and desperately tried to recover it after it was lost, but his efforts were wholly vain. This too, was the first open field fight of the campaign, and for us the most complete victory as yet gained. The entire loss of the Thirty-Eighth during the two days fighting was two killed, four wounded—one mortally—and one missing. All the men lost during the fight were lost from rear or flank firing, from which the men quickly protected themselves as soon as opportunity offered.

Leaving the railroad the regiment moved a short distance towards the Yellow House, where it encamped and fortified its position in front, flank and rear.

CHAPTER VII.

On the 29th of August, while the regiment was out performing picket duty, orders were unexpectedly received for the regiment to break camp, and soon as relieved, to follow the Brigade, with all possible speed, in the direction of Reams' Station, seven miles distant. The column took the double-quick, and constantly urged forward, kept up its speed until it arrived on the field of battle. Many of the men had become exhausted by the way and were compelled to fall out; but the remainder, though few in number, and having been only an hour in marching the distance, immediately moved into line so as to close a gap between the Second and Fifth Corps.

The fighting, however, had nearly ceased, and soon quieted down altogether. The day following, the battalion moved several miles to the right, and took part in the work of extending the chain of forts and line of breastworks along the front of the ground acquired and held by our forces. During the month fatigue duty of every nature was performed. Earthworks extending miles in length, with double and often treble rows of abattis in front, bridges, railroads and corduroy roads, were built, the work being pushed forward day and night, rainy or fair weather, Sundays as well as week days, without intermission

Camps were formed; company and brigade drills were had; mounting of brigade and other general guards were instituted, and the *morale* of the army generally, greatly improved after these victories.

Alarms and anticipated attacks were frequent, such as any soldier of experience will readily understand, usually resulting in the batteries opening and shelling furiously for an hour or so ; but the murderous picket firing, so common in the immediate front of Petersburg, was entirely wanting here. Quartermasters and Sutlers came up from City Point and joined their commands—the weather grew a little cooler—grand news came up from Sheridan, and everything assumed a brighter, more cheering, and more prosperous aspect.

On the 25th of September a new movement was inaugurated. Relieved by colored troops, the regiment moved off the line and took a four days' rest, and then started again on the war-path. On the 29th the Ninth Corps moved near to the Wilson House, and there lay and listened to the engagement between the Fifth Corps and the enemy.

Prisoners and the wounded began streaming toward the rear, and, as usual in such cases, rumors were rife as to how the fight was going. The next day the Ninth Corps moved forward to engage the enemy. Early the men had been aroused; coffee was boiled, tents rolled up, and the column marched toward the theatre of yesterday's fight. Passing Poplar Spring Church, the battalion emerged from the woods and took position on the "Pegram Plantation." After waiting about an hour, orders came for the brigade commanded by Col. Harriman to

move forward and engage the enemy. A field battery was already shelling the woods where the hidden enemy lay. Moving the brigade by the right flank, in a line perpendicular to the enemy's front, the brigade, by a halt, front, and right wheel, swung around into line. The Thirty-Eighth was detached from the left of the brigade and moved to the right, to support a battery. The fight began and raged furiously for a short time. Suddenly the regiments on the left began to break and scatter; the panic extended from regiment to regiment, and like a tumbling row of blocks, the line crumbled, broke and scattered toward the rear, leaving the Thirty-Eighth alone with the battery. Flanked on its right and left, with an enemy flushed with success and an assurance of victory, the position of the battalion was precarious in the extreme. Though numbering only about one hundred and fifty men, all told, it steadily held the enemy in check until the artillery had time to limber up and move off the field. Then it gradually fell back, in good style, until it reached the wood, where it took up a position, which it held until the next morning. Here the glad news was received that Col. Bintliff, with five companies, and a detachment to strengthen the others, had arrived. A few hours after, the new battalion arrived at the position, and the two battalions were merged together.

CHAPTER VIII.

It was expected and earnestly hoped, by Col. Bintliff and the other officers of the Thirty-Eighth, who were obliged to remain in the State when the first battalion left, that the regiment would be filled and the balance soon be able to go forward and take the field; but circumstances were unpropitious, a variety of causes conspiring to delay that consummation. The State had nearly filled its quota, under the pending call of the President for men for the military service of the country; and that, coupled with the interest that an almost exclusively agricultural people always feel, at seeding time, in their labors, tended to withdraw the attention of the people, in a great measure, from the contemplation of the great struggle. Add to this, that our young State had already met, and, from her sparse population, filled all calls upon her for men, until the drain began to be severely felt in every walk of life, and it will not appear at all surprising that recruiting lagged, and but few men were enlisted during the summer of 1864.

Company E was finally raised, and organized in June. On the 20th of July the company left Madison for the theater of active service. It arrived in front of Petersburg and joined the four companies that had

preceded it, on the 26th of the same month, taking part and suffering severely in the battle of the Mined Fort on the 30th. It was in this battle that its Captain, N. S. Ferris, a noble and true man, was killed.

In this manner the spring passed and the summer wore on until the 18th of July, when the President issued his proclamation of that date, calling for 500,-000 more men, with the alternative of a draft in case any state failed to fill its quota within fifty days after the issuing of the proclamation. Nor, even then, did recruiting quickly revive. The call came just at the time when the farmers of the Northwest were the most heavily engaged in harvesting their crops. But in August the great mass of the people became thoroughly aroused, and fully appreciated the necessities of the situation. Men from all the walks of life cast aside every consideration of home comforts, business and all ties, and unreservedly gave themselves to the army and to filling up its wasted ranks. Large local bounties were offered, and meetings were held in almost every school house, at which spirited addresses were made. The feeling of the people, while it was not so wildly enthusiastic as in 1861, was equally intense and determined. By the middle of September, the Thirty-Eighth was filled. The class of men recruited for it was such as drew encomiums from all.

On the 20th, the last company was fully organized; and on the 22nd, at 8 o'clock A. M., the battalion left Camp Randall and started for the seat of war. The following letter gives a very fair description of the journey from Madison, until the battalion reached "the front" and there joined the first battalion.

Mr. Editor :—The Thirty-Eighth regiment broke camp at Madison, on the 22d of September, and started for Dixie. The day was pleasant, the accommodations comfortable, and the boys, nearly all, in the gayest of spirits. It is true a few, as their thoughts reverted to home and the loved ones, they were leaving for the field of danger, perhaps never to return, would allow a not unmanly tear to dim their eyes for a moment.

About 10 o'clock, A. M., the whistle shrieked its shrill note of warning—the conductor and company officers shouted their " all aboard," and we were off for the city of " mud and effluvia." Only one of our company deserted, and he on the morning we left Madison. His name is Henry T. Lawrence. He was from Lindon, Juneau county. Our journey to Chicago was, on the whole, a pleasant one. Everywhere along the route we were greeted by the waving of handkerchiefs and hats. We arrived at Chicago about 11 o'clock, P. M., and immediately marched to the Park, opposite the Soldier's Rest, where we bivouaced for the remainder of the night. In the morning a good and wholesome breakfast was served up to the boys at the Rest, to which they did ample justice.

With three rousing cheers, such as we Badgers are wont to give when we feel it, for the Soldier's Rest of Chicago, we started for Pittsburg, via Ft. Wayne and Crestline. Our journey was not so pleasant this day, for the clouds which had been thickening since early morning, about 10 o'clock opened their floodgates and the rain descended almost in torrents. That evening in a heavy, driving rain, we arrived at

Ft. Wayne, where we stopped long enough to get
supper. The next morning, in time for an early
breakfast, we reached Crestline, and the next evening Pittsburg. Immediately on leaving the cars at
the latter place, we marched to the Soldier's Rest,
where we found a supper, that would have been a
credit to any hotel in the land, awaiting the demands
of our appetites, made ravenous by three days of
travel. And here let me stop to add my tribute of
praise to that spirit of liberality and patriotism
which, from the beginning of this unhappy contest,
has been displayed by the citizens of Pittsburg, and
which must carve for it a broad niche in the grateful remembrance of future generations, as it already
has in the remembrance of this. This Soldier's Rest,
at which every regiment of Union troops that passes
through Pittsburg is fed at least one meal, was established in August, 1861, and has ever since been
sustained entirely by the private contributions of the
citizens of that city. All honor to their noble patri-
otic generosity!

I wish that truth would admit of my speaking in
even terms of commendation of the Pennsylvania
railroad, but I must confess my belief that it is the
meanest, dirtiest, and most soulless corporation on
the face of God's footstool. If there is one that de-
serves more execration, may Heaven pity the poor
soldier who is obliged to pass over it. A majority
of our men were huddled together in freight cars,
and in these, without fires or light of any kind, were
dragged at a snail's pace through the chilling and
benumbing night air of the Allegany mountains.
We arrived at Altoona, in the mountains, in time for

breakfast, and at 9 o'clock that morning again started on our way. Creeping and winding around the mountains, or speeding down some narrow ravine, we struck, before dark, the broad valley of the Susquehanna river. Turning off six miles west of Harrisburg, the Capital of Pennsylvania, we were on the road to Baltimore, now, thank God, by the free untrammeled act of the citizens of beautiful Maryland, a free city in a free State. The experience of the night before had notified us of the kind of treatment we might expect from the Pennsylvania railroad, on which we were still traveling, and a few of us determined not to submit to it. Night of Egpytian darkness came on, but with it came no lights or fuel from the railroad company, to light or warm up the cars. Western spunk and spirit would not submit to it longer. Captain Coleman, than whom a better soldier or finer gentleman is not, and the writer, applied to Col. Bintliff for leave to bring the railroad company to a sense of duty. Leave was readily granted. On arriving at York a soldier was stationed at each brake with orders as soon as the train stopped to put on the brakes and under no circumstances, to let them up until ordered by some officer of the regiment. The conductor was notified to produce light and that the train should not stir an inch until the notice was complied with. Of course there was considerable bluster, but we told them that as the train lay on the track so no others could pass, if the company could afford to have all its trains blocked there, we could afford to wait for morning and daylight, *and would.* In a short time lights were forthcoming—the cars were lighted up—the brakes

E

let up, and we were again on our way to Baltimore, where we arrived next morning.

A breakfast, the smell of which alone vanquished your correspondent and almost the entire 38th, and drove it in disorder into the street, was served to us at the Soldiers' Rest. We understand this is a government institution, run on contract. I think so, for the food seemed to have *contracted* all the odors of all the filth of the city. A restaurant supplied many of us with a palatable meal. Here, also, we had a sight of some nine hundred rebel prisoners, captured by Sheridan in the Shenandoah Valley. They were a good looking lot of men, but very meanly clothed.

After a rest of two or three hours, we took the cars for Washington, where we arrived, without the occurrence of any incident worth noting, that afternoon, and immediately marched to the barracks. The next day we received our arms—the Springfield rifled musket. The next day we went aboard the Steamboat John A. Warner, and about noon were really off for Dixie, and that line, so little comprehended by our people at home, "the front." On Thursday morning, September 29th, just one week from the time we left Madison, we passed Fort Monroe, and the next evening reached City Point, the headquarters of Gen. Grant. We stayed aboard the boat that night, and the next (Friday) morning went ashore and lay there till about noon, when orders came for us to take cars and report to Gen. Meade, or somebody else, away to the south of Petersburg. The day was showery, but nothing seemed to dampen the spirits of our noble boys. Just at dark we

reached the end of the railroad, and after waiting about an hour for orders, were marched back nearly two miles to the Yellow House, near which we encamped for the night. The night was dark and rainy, the roads muddy, and, of course, the march hard and very disagreeable. Two or three of the boys, under the accumulated load of gun, shelter tent, haversack, canteen, and very plethoric knapsack, gave out on the march, but came up a short time afterwards.

On Saturday afternoon we reached the camp of that part of the 38th which had preceded us, and were warmly greeted by our "veteran brothers in arms." Hardly had the boys unslung their knapsacks, when the rebels sent a shell howling over our heads, and sharp picket firing was heard in front. Preparations were immediately made to repel any attack, but the rebels, mindful of the previous day's chastisement on this very ground, and probably discovering that our forces had thrown up formidable breastworks during the night, thought discretion the better part of valor, and retired without further demonstration. That some of our men were somewhat excited, was no more than was to be expected, but none were extremely so.

That night we camped on the ground, thoroughly drenched as it was with the previous rain. The next morning was clear and beautiful; and this, our first Sabbath in Virginia, promised to be, indeed, for us a day of rest. Clothes were spread out to dry, fires were built, and every one proceeded to make himself as comfortable as possible.

In the evening, however, came orders to move. Our lines were to be advanced, and strong earth-

works thrown up, and the 38th was to take a hand
in. Moving a mile or so to our right, we halted,
arms were stacked, the several regiments divided
into reliefs, and the work commenced. Daylight
found the 38th behind a strong line of breastworks.
It was here that private Simpson was injured by a
falling tree. He is now in hospital, but much better.
From this time on, until about a week since, no regiment was ever more over-worked and subjected to
exposure than ours. As might have been expected,
this course sent nearly or quite one-third of the men
into the hospital. I do not pretend to say where the
blame lies, but there is some one who has little less
than the guilt of murder on his soul. Now, however,
all is changed. Through the efforts of Col. Bintliff,
the men have been relieved from overtaxing duties,
and, as a consequence, feel re-invigorated and more
hopeful.   KRIEG.

From the first of October until late in the month,
these constant and overtaxing duties were required.
Nearly or quite one-third of the regiment were sent
out on picket daily, while almost an equal number
were detailed for camp guard. This kind of duty
would only allow the men one night's rest in three.
Even those men who were exempt for the day from
picket or camp guard, were required to perform
fatigue duties, company, battalion, and brigade drills
or Dress Parade. Such a senseless and inhuman
course could have but one result. The men, worn out
by exposure and fatigue, became a prey to all the ills
consequent to a malarious climate. In a few weeks
two-thirds of the command were either in the hospital,
or excused by the Surgeon from duty.

CHAPTER IX.

In the meantime the movement of the 27th of October was inaugurated. The previous evening Col. Bintliff called the company officers to Regimental Headquarters, and informed them that a movement was in progress, and that the Thirty-Eighth would move at two o'clock next morning. He informed them that a battle was expected to follow as a result of the movement, and said he had been informed that the Thirty-Eighth would be assigned to an honorable position in the coming fight. Said he felt extremely anxious that the Regiment should behave in a creditable manner; and reminded those present that, on *their* conduct in leading, would depend almost entirely the good behavior and efficiency of the enlisted men ; and hoped all would act with coolness, bravery and discretion.

The officers returned to their respective quarters, and immediately the busy hum of preparation was heard throughout the camp. Five day's rations were cooked and issued to the men. Knapsacks were packed, and at two o'clock A. M. of October 27th, the Regiment was ready to move. Moving along our lines to the left to the distance of a half mile or so, the Regiment passed out through the works of the Third

Division, to the front, and after marching a short distance halted to allow other troops to file past.

For nearly an hour the Regiment lay where it was
halted, while regiment after regiment filed past it.
Finally it again moved toward the front. Daylight
came and we were still moving off to the left and
front. About seven o'clock the crack of musketry
was heard along our skirmish line—our skirmishers
had discovered the enemy's pickets and were driving
them in. Still mile after mile, over fields and through
woods and brush, moving by the flank, the Regiment
kept on its way. The fire on the skirmish line
gradually increased as we neared the enemy's main
line of works. Reaching a strip of timber that partially
hid our men from the view of the enemy, the Regiment was halted and thrown into line of battle, in the
rear of two other lines. Suddenly on the right the
heavy boom of artillery was heard, and shell came
howling and thundering along our ranks. The enemy
had discovered our position, and had opened with a
battery in a position to rake our whole line. Under
these trying circumstances the men lay as coolly and
quietly, almost, as though they were in camp.

After laying in this situation for about an hour,
orders came for the Regiment to move to the left and
take a new position. While executing this movement, a shell came crashing through the Regiment
and knocked down two ranks of double files of
company G. Only one of the men, David Harned,
was seriously injured; the rest gathered up their guns
and accoutrements and coolly took their places in
the ranks. With scarcely a halt for this incident,
the Regiment moved on thirty or forty rods, when it

was brought to a front, and moved up into the front line of battle. It was getting to be warm out on the skirmish lines, and the bullets were whistling through the air in a very lively manner. To increase the uncomfortableness of the situation, the battery that had been throwing shells along the line, now changed and threw grape and canister. Suddenly a cheer broke out far to the right, there were a few rapid discharges of artillery, and then, comparatively, all was quiet again. The rebel battery had ceased to pay its attentions to us and become silent.

That the cheer and the silence of the battery were in some way connected, seemed evident, nor did we have to wait long for an explanation. A brigade of Negro troops had been ordered to charge the battery, and going in in splendid style, had compelled the rebels to limber up, and get away on a run, to save their guns from being captured.

Relieved from the troublesome attentions of the rebel battery, the Thirty-Eighth quietly remained in its assigned position, expecting each moment an order to advance. News came from the extreme left that affairs were prospering finely with the Second and Fifth Corps, and the men felt in good temper for the work they expected to soon be called upon to perform. But the day wore away, and no orders to move came. The afternoon had been slightly showery, and as the day drew to a close the heavens became thickly overcast, and a heavy rain commenced falling. The skirmish line was strongly reinforced, a guard detailed along the line, and the balance of the regiment—each man protecting himself as best he could, and wrapping himself in his

blanket—lay down and slept as soundly and sweetly there, in the immediate presence of the enemy, and in a drenching rain, as the more favored ones at the North, whose limbs were pillowed on beds of down.

Toward morning a light breeze sprung up, and the clouds began to break away, although it still rained at intervals.

At daylight all were aroused, coffee boiled and breakfast eaten. Then with such few tools as could be obtained, the men were set to work to erect breastworks. Logs, poles, rails, brush, leaves, and in fact everything that could be obtained, that would assist to turn a bullet, was brought into use.

Rumor, too, began to peddle unwelcome news. It was said that our forces on the left had met with a severe check.

A little later, and it was whispered around that the left wing was rapidly falling back. The report proved true.

The Thirty-Eighth, which had for some time been standing under arms, was brought to an about-face and moved to the rear. Falling back a short distance, to some partially constructed works, the regiment was again faced to the front.

All this time there was continuous and heavy firing on the skirmish line. Waiting a few moments for some troops to pass to the rear, the regiment again fell back a short distance, and again formed in line of battle, and faced to the enemy. This movement was repeated several times, until all apprehension of pursuit being over, the regiment moved back to camp, where it arrived about four o'clock in the afternoon.

The principal cause of this check to the movement seems to have arisen from the Second and Fifth corps failing to connect. Through the gap that intervened between the two commands, the rebels succeeded in throwing a heavy force, which, falling on the flank of the Second corps, doubled it up and threw it into inextricable confusion.

The Fifth corps also suffered severely from the same cause. After that, it became evident that the movement could not be continued without a loss too heavy to be commensurated by the object to be obtained, and so it was abandoned, and the great "reconnoisance in force" came to an end.

CHAPTER X.

On the return of the regiment to camp, the same routine of duties and labors, that prevailed previous to leaving it, were again established, and the "sick list" swelled its enormous proportions. The surgeon remonstrated earnestly against the continuance of a system that had already sent two-thirds of the command to the hospital, and large numbers to the grave. Col. Bintliff, too, took hold of the matter and represented to Brigade Headquarters the magnitude of the evil that was being inflicted on the men. Finally, about the middle of November, these efforts were successful, and the condition of the men sensibly ameliorated. The amount of guard duty on picket was considerably decreased, the camp guard was cut down from seventy-five to about twenty men, and the amount of fatigue labor required, lessened nearly or quite one half. The beneficial effects of this change were felt almost immediately. The number of sick reporting to the surgeon shortly began to fall off and lessened daily. On the daily drills the men moved with energy, instead of the feeble lassitude that had previously characterized their actions; and it is doubtful if the spirit and efficiency of the regiment had at any time previously equalled that exhibited during the last few days of

its stay near Peeble's House. The following letter gives a very truthful relation of the matters of which it speaks:

Camp near Peeble's House, Va., }
Tuesday, Nov. 15th, 1864.   }

DEAR PRESS:—As the telegraph used, during the lifetime of "Little Mac," and while he controled the operations of our armies, to daily chronicle the fact that all was "quiet on the Potomac," so I have nothing of importance to communicate to your readers, save that quiet reigns, all along the lines of our army, on the James river and in front of Petersburg.

The election here was probably as free and untrammeled an expression of the will of the soldiers voting, as ever was given by an equal number of men, at any time, in our country. Many of the company commanders went through their respective companies with Union tickets in one hand, and McClellan and Pendleton tickets in the other, and freely distributed them among their men, at the same time charging them that in the exercise of the great right of suffrage, they were acting solely in their capacity as American citizens, and as such, to vote for those whom they believed would administer the Government, during the next four years, for the best interest of the nation. The charge, made by some of the unscrupulous copperhead papers, that regiments were paraded and marched by their officers up to the polls, and directed to vote for Lincoln, is simply an absolute, unqualified falsehood. So far as my observation extended, not only were the men not paraded at the polls that day, but, with the exception of camp guard and picket duty, they were excused

from all duties until "Dress Parade," at 4 o'clock in the afternoon—long before which every man had cast his ballot.

Over the result of the recent election, the rebels feel quite as blue as their brother copperheads of the North. There was this difference between these two classes, however—the rebs really believed that Little Mac had a good chance for the election, and that his success was equivalent to an acknowledgement of their independence, while the copperheads of the North, for the purpose of securing the votes of the War Democracy and inveigling the unwary into supporting their ticket, dishonestly pretended to be sanguine of McClellan's election, and that his election was synonymous with peace and a restored Union. Of course the great body of the two classes are bitterly disappointed. A little incident, that occured almost in our immediate front, will illustrate, in some measure, the disappointment of the rebs. The picket lines of the opposing armies are within a few rods of each other; so near indeed, that the videttes can readily talk to each other. Three or four days after the election a newsboy came along our picket crying out his papers. One of the Johnnies, anxious to hear of the success of McClellan, of which, it seems, he had no doubt, hallooed to the newsboy and asked him how election had gone. "Big for Lincoln," was the reply. "Its a G—d d——d lie," shouted the reb in the bitterness of his disappointment; and then a little squad of them were seen to gather together, and if gestures are any indication, earnestly dicuss the news.

Another incident is equally instructive and inter-

esting. It was told me by an officer, who witnessed it, and whose words need no voucher. When the newspapers were first received here containing the evidence of Lincoln's re-election, one of our officers took one and went out between the lines, (a thing practiced almost every day,) to exchange papers with the rebs. He was met there by a rebel Captain, anxious for a trade which was soon consummated. The rebel anxiously looked over the election returns, until convinced that Lincoln was really elected, when he threw the paper on the ground and actually shed tears. In the subsequent conversation it appeared that he had believed in the election of McClellan and the consequent acknowledgment of the independence of the confederacy. Now, however, he frankly admitted that the South had no hope but to make the best terms she could, and submit to the power of the Federal government.

The 38th, since my last, has had no experience but such as is incident to the camp life of the soldier. Relieved from the overburdening tasks imposed upon it during the first four weeks after our arrival here, and aided by the cool weather, the health of the whole regiment, here in camp, is much improved. Our men owe a debt of gratitude to Surgeon Russell for his efficient and untiring zeal for their welfare. In these days of drunken, careless and inefficient Surgeons, it is a pleasure, as well as a duty, to acknowledge the merit of those who really devote themselves to the work of relieving the sufferings of the sick and wounded soldiers. Dr. Russell is from Fox Lake, Dodge county.

The field officers of the regiment are men who

grow in one's good graces, the longer he is acquainted with them. Col. Bintliff, although a strict disciplinarian, is very careful for the welfare of his men.

Lieut. Col. Pier has been in command of the first five organized companies of the 38th, during the spring and summer campaign. He is a fine appearing, social gentleman, and his companions speak in very flattering terms of his soldierly qualities.

Maj. Roberts and Adjutant McCracken have each earned honors on the field, and are first rate fellows.

KRIEG.

On the 29th of November, the Ninth Corps broke camp and moved into the trenches immediately in front of Petersburg. The part occupied by the first division extended from the Norfolk and Petersburg Railroad to the Appomattox River. The Thirty-Eighth was posted on the extreme left of the line occupied by the division. This position it held until the capture of Petersburg, on the morning of the 2d of April, 1865.

The regiment arrived upon the ground assigned, just after dark.

The following letter will give some incidents of interest that occurred at this time:

In the Trenches before Petersburg, ⟩
Dec. 8th, 1864. ⟨

DEAR PRESS:—Since my last, the 38th regiment has again "changed its base," and moved much nearer to that city which remains to be entered by those of the great army of the Potomac who continue faithful to our cause, and hold out to the end—*i. e.* Petersburg.

The distance from our former camp to Petersburg

was nearly or quite seven miles. From our present position it is not over two and a half or three miles: the church steeples and spires being in plain view, as would also be the city, but for a high ridge between our lines and that place. On the crest and outer slope of the ridge, the rebs have constructed three lines of earthworks, which, so far, have proved very serious obstacles to our peaceable entry into the city; a piece of vain foolishness on their part, which shall surely be brought to nothing; for hath not Ulysses said it!

The prospect before us is decidedly muddy. If there is a "soger" in the 38th who doesn't feel, and look too, as though he had put his foot into it, the subscriber has failed to discover him.

At any rate, all who traverse our rather extended picket line through the slush, in many places over knee deep, will feel the force, if they fail to see the "pint." On the 29th of November last, we broke up our beautiful camp at Peeble's House, and marched to the position we now occupy. The march, though not a long one, owing to the state of the roads, rendered in many places almost impassable by the late heavy rains, was fatiguing in the extreme, obliging many of the men to fall out on the way. We arrived at this place in the evening, about 8 o'clock, and slept on the ground, with nothing but our blankets for protection.   *   *   *   *   *   *   *

The weather is very fine and invigorating, and the health and strength of the army is very much improved under its favorable influences.   KRIEG.

The next day after the arrival of the Regiment in the position assigned it, the camp was laid out, tent-

erected and everything made as comfortable as possible. On the picket lines, however, a murderous fire was kept up night and day. On either side a dozen bullets were sent at every indication of life in the opposing lines. In this way the pickets of our Regiment expended from 2,000 to 10,000 rounds of ammunition daily. The bullets of the enemy, in answer, whistled and purred over our main line. Almost every day some one was wounded or killed. The trained marksmen of Wisconsin, however, were sure to repay the enemy, *in kind*, with large measure for every injury of this kind inflicted upon us.

Here, too, almost every day we were obliged to submit to the uncomfortable artillery practice of the enemy. Yet, notwithstanding these difficulties in the way, battalion and brigade drills were kept up almost daily. Ditches were dug, new covered ways constructed, and old works enlarged, repaired and strengthened. Without cessation, through all the month of December, these labors and duties were performed by the men. The rains of December filled the ditches with water, and hundreds of feet continually worked, and ground and mixed it with earth, until the ditches and pits became so many mortar beds. The men literally waded, stood, sat and slept in the mud. But amid all the uncomfortableness of the situation, the men, encouraged by the glorious news from Thomas, Sherman and the Atlantic seaboard, endured everything with an heroic fortitude that could but win the admiration and praise of all.

On the 23d of December, Pound Sterling wrote as follows to the State *Journal:*

F

"Trenches before Petersburg, Virginia,
December 23d, 1864.

The echo of news swells into one grand anthem of victory. We received the telegraphic dispatches this morning, officially signed. If the news is glorious to you at home, what must it be to the soldier who sees in it the glimmer of the hope he had not till now dared to cherish—that of sitting down some happy day in the midst of that group of loved and joyous faces in his own home! That's what makes victory glorious.

It is needless to repeat the news: The fall of Savannah—the destruction of Hood—Wilmington threatened—Charleston and Augusta threatened—Mobile threatened—Breckenridge overwhelmed—a cloud of war and famine hovering over Richmond!

The reserve line of battle has heard the news; the front line has heard it; the pickets have heard it; and ever since dawn, cheer after cheer has rent the air. The soldiers salute each other this morning with, "Hurrah for home!" "How are you, Jeff. Davis!" "How are you, Southern Confederacy!" "I don't want a furlough!" I tell you, Mr. Editor, we feel *decidedly good.*

When national good news flood the press, regimental affairs sink into insignificance. But I'll venture to say a word to let our friends know that 'we still live.' There have been few casualties since my last. This is due to the energy displayed by the regiment in fitting up the picket line. Sharpshooters annoyed us very much at first, but now we have covered ways to the line, and casualties need only occur

by shells and carelessness. Picket firing has abated somewhat, but there was a lively fusillade last night. Occasionally a sharp artillery fire fills the air with bursting shells. Deserters come in every night in squads of men from two to half a dozen. They report universal dissatisfaction among the rebel troops. One party threw down their guns in presence of the officer of the picket line and pickets, and walked over to our posts. They say their whole Brigade will come before long. Officers and men talk of the waning fortunes of the Confederacy, and universally decide that "it is going to h—l." Three came in this morning: They confirm the report that Lee is wounded, and that one of our shells killed their chief of artillery on the 16th. They report rations short, as usual in such cases. But what they say of poor and insufficient clothing is thought to be true. 'And many such little things they say.' * * *
* * * * *

Col. Bintliff has returned to the command of the regiment. He has for some time been in command of the Third Brigade. Capt. Ballard, Co. A, has gone home on furlough. There have been several of late in the regiment, but it would be needless to name them, as you are are always ahead of correspondents in looking after such matters. I hope to have something good to write in my next.

£."

During all this time, and until the 9th of January, 1863, the same murderous picket fire that had previously prevailed, was contantly kept up. Through the nights, while darkness protected the men from the fatal and deadly aim of the enemy's sharpshoot-

ers, fatigue parties were constantly at work. Ditches were dug, breastworks thrown up, pits constructed and gabions manufactured, and so placed as to protect all exposed points, until our picket line became almost absolutely safe from every thing but shells. About this time a "flag of truce" came over from the rebels. Some of the ladies of Secessia, having tired of the luxuries of rebellion, anxiously desired to come through the lines and once more place themselves beneath the protecting folds of the National flag. The ceremony was winessed by thousands on each side. After some delay, the application was refused, and these fair sinners learned once more that the " way of the transgressor is hard."

CHAPTER XI.

On the 9th of January, one of those heavy storms, uncommonly heavy in this instance, prevailed during the day and night. The ground became deluged with water and sleet, and the ditches were literally filled with it. In some instances the men were obliged to stand for hours in water and mud nearly knee deep. Banks caved off, and breastworks, the labor of weeks and months, were washed down in a few hours. On the morning of the 10th, by mutual consent, the opposing forces ceased firing on each other, and quietly proceeded to rebuild and repair their respective works.

KRIEG has hardly overdrawn the picture in the following letter witten at that time:

DEAR PRESS:—Mud, mud, mud is now king in Virginia, and for the last thirty-six hours the nasty monarch has been holding complete sway through all the camps, trenches, pits and covered ways of the Army of the Potomac. Mud saturated soldiers, wading through trenches of almost bottomless mud, with muddy hands salute mud covered officers as deep in the mud as themselves; and considerate foes refuse to fire on each other, because they are unable to tell, with anything like accuracy, where in the vast heap of moving mud, the incarnate enemy is located.

Since my last, few changes have occured in the Thirty-Eighth regiment. Capt. Cory, of company H, has been discharged for disability. Capt. Coleman, of company I, is at home sick, on Leave of Absence. Lt. Col. Pier is at home, on Leave of Absence, enjoying the rest and pleasure to which his arduous duties during the spring and summer campaign, ably performed, fully entitled him. This morning Col. Bintliff left the regiment for Washington, and is expected to be absent four days. The Col. was accompanied on his way by Major Roberts and Capt. Hayward who go home on a twenty day's visit. These changes for the time being, placed Capt. Kelly, of company F, in command 'of the regiment with Capt. Marsden next in rank.

During the six weeks our regiment has occupied its present position, the proximity of our line of pickets, to the enemy's works, subjects our men to an almost continual fire from the enemy's pickets and sharpshooters, and yet we have lost, so excellent are our works, only four men killed and five wounded. None of company K have been injured.

It seems almost providential that no more of our men are injured by the fire of the enemy; for, certainly, no troops have ever shown a more hardy—I had almost said reckless—contempt for personal danger. The very opposite is the case with the enemy, as they keep themselves well covered by their works. I remarked the difference to a deserter a few nights since, and asked him the cause. "We 'uns have nobody to put in his place, if one of our fellers gets killed, as you 'uns have," was the sententious reply. Our regiment has received quite an acces-

tion to its numbers fit for duty, during the last week,
in convalescents returned from various hospitals.

Yours truly,   KRIEG.

While matters were progressing thus quietly, one
of those incidents occurred that, while it was of no
particular importance in itself, served for the moment
to relieve the dull monotony of camp life. A woman,
whose husband had deserted from the rebel army
and succeeded in reaching our lines, had made application to the Rebel Commander to obtain permission
for herself to pass through the line, that she might be
able to join her husband who was then in Government employ at Norfolk.

Owing, perhaps, to the fact that a similar application, under flag of truce, had been denied by the
Federal Commander but a few days previously, Gen.
Lee refused the request, but intimated that if she
could succeed in working her way through the lines
he would have no objection to her doing so. With
this slight encouragement the courageous woman determined to make the effort. An influential friend
accompanied her as far as the rebel picket line and
succeeded in obtaining permission for her to pass
through. It must have been a most trying moment
to her. Behind she was leaving home, friends and
all the scenes and associations of her life. The ties
of kindred were to be severed, perhaps never to be
linked again. Before her everything was wrapped in
uncertainty, except danger. But behind, also, was
grim want and stern oppression, while before her was,
at least, the hope of again joining her husband and
enjoying peace, quiet and plenty.

So, buoyed up by this hope, she bade her friend

"good-bye," took her little child of two years in her arms, and resolutely turned her face toward the Union lines. Hundreds on either side watched her progress as she slowly and laboriously traversed the space between the opposing lines. When she arrived within a few rods of our works, a gallant Union soldier sprang over them and, going to her assistance, relieved her of her burthen and brought it into our lines. Assured by the kindly manner in which she had been received, the woman told her sad story of destitution and her final determination to seek relief, by gaining admission within our lines, with the hope of finding her husband.

The regulations, however, required that her case should be passed upon and decided at Army Headquarters, before she could be allowed to proceed farther. A delay of several hours took place; but, meanwhile, every pains were taken to render her enforced delay as comfortable as possible. The "boys," with a spirit of generous hospitality, always a part of the nature of a true soldier, feasted her and her child on the choicest "hardtack," and the finest coffee they could prepare. Finally, orders were received to admit her, and she was forwarded, just before night, first to Brigade, and then to Division Headquarters where accommodations were furnished her for the night. The next morning she was forwarded to her destination.

Meanwhile the glorious tidings from Georgia and the Carolinas increased in grandeur and importance. Our soldiers were elated with the news. A hearty enthusiasm pervaded every portion and rank of the army. The same causes that inspired and raised the

spirits of our men, served in a corresponding measure to depress those of the enemy. Desertions, which before had been numerous, now increased to such an extent that the rebels came over, not singly as formerly, but in squads.

Then came the news of the failure of the Wilmington expedition, under the command of Gen. Butler. For a short time the tables seemed turned against us. Yet for all that, though our men seemed somewhat depressed in spirit, and the rebels quite jubilant over the result, it was noticed that there was very little falling off, in the number of deserters. But a few days elapsed, however, before the news of the success of Gen. Terry and Commodore Porter, in capturing Fort Fisher and closing the port of Wilmington, removed every vestige of gloom from the minds of our soldiers, and sent the spirits of the rebels into a state of despondency anything but agreeable. Salutes were fired from our batteries, and cheers on cheers rang along our lines. Yet it must be confessed that the rebels bore their tribulations with surprising fortitude "You'll break your necks yet in some of your moves! Old Bobby is only giving you a little rope," said a rebel one day across the line. "If we do there'll be life enough left to pound your Confederacy into the earth," was the prompt reply of a Union soldier.

We find the following letter relating to affairs at this time in the State *Journal :*

"Headquarters 1st Brig. 1st Div. 9th A. C., }
Before Petersburg, Jan. 17th, 1865. }

Startling events burst so continuously upon us that we have hardly time to swing our hats and

hurrah for one, before another comes.   The echo of
the salute given in honor of Sherman's 'Christmas
Gift'—has hardly died away, when again the cannon thunders a welcome to the news from Fort Fisher.
The news was immediately ordered to be taken to
'Johnny rebs.'   Col. Harriman also sent the brigade
band to the front, to give them a few national airs.
Mingled with this, cheer after cheer went up from
thousands of joyful soldiers.   Some of the rebs
at first did not seem to like it, but many of them appeared as much pleased over it as we.   Col. Bintliff went down to the picket line to break the news to
the rebs in our immediate front.   After he had announced it, he asked them how they liked *that*.
'Bully for you!' says one.   'That's bully!' said
another.   A third added 'Fort Fisher's nothing!'
'Richmond's nothing!'   If all that is true, I would
like to have some Copperhead banker compute the
interest for one year in Confederate scrip, on one
thousand dollars, and tell me the value in gold.   It
wouldn't sum up enough to buy his boy Pete a 'ca-
nine jack-knife.'

Your Johnny rebels have just come over and have
been put through the 'pickets' pretty well, Cols.
Harriman and Bintliff, Majors Smith and Eaton, and
Captains Norton and Hobbs, constituting the board
of investigation.   They confirm the rumor in refer-
ence to the Union proclivities of Georgia.   One of
them is from that State, and says he *knows* the people
of Georgia will hail with joy the return of the old
flag, and will do all in their power to restore the
Union.   He renewed the complaint of insufficient
rations, 'and then,' he said 'you can buy nothing

with a moderate amount of Confederate money.'
He pointed to a pair of cavalry boots an officer was
wearing, and said 'such would cost five hundred
dollars in Petersburg. Coarse shoes cost fifty dollars. Bob. Lee is a great general, but Grant has
fronted him on every flank. There is universal dissatisfaction among our men. They do not want to
fight any more. Lee dare not attempt to retreat, as
it would divide his army. One half would go to the
front, (to the Union army.) My regiment pickets in
front of the 'Crater' and to the right. Bob. Lee
has told the people of Petersburg and Richmond,
that if they don't furnish the army with rations, he
must and will take his army away in three weeks, and
the people are anxious for him to do so, as his im-
pressments for food are *starving* them. Oh, sir, you
can have no idea of the deep settled misery and despair that this war has brought upon Virginia. I belong to an Alabama brigade, but I am from the
State of Georgia. I *know* the people of Georgia will
shout for joy at the return of the State to the Union.'
He made the same assertion of the people of Petersburg. 'The report reached our camps to-day, that
Gov. Thomas Watts, of Alabama, had resigned. I
know the Governor, and know him to be a Union
man at heart. He would not furnish any more men
to the Confederacy. It was also reported to-day
that Fort Fisher is captured.'

This man was intelligent and seemed to belong to
the better class. He gave much other information
and other incidents; told the names of men in his
regiment who had made a special mark of some of our
officers while on the picket line. They spoke feelingly

of friends they had left in the army and told amusing incidents of the picket line and of their escape.

I have never seen a deeper depression of spirit among the rebels than there seems to be at present, nor a more jubilant and confident spirit among our men. There has been no firing to amount to anything since the flag of truce attempted to bring over the ladies; General Meade, unnatural man, would not allow them to come. Both armies have improved the opportunity to fit up the picket lines and breastworks. The Colonel in command of the brigade, Col. Harriman, has bent every energy to the work and our pickets are now comfortable and safe. But we were a very sorry looking set, I assure you, during and after the terrible thunder storm of the night of the 9th inst.

Picture yourself a second Horace Greeley crouched in a picket pit within a few rods of the enemy, wincing beneath the falling torrents of cold rain; his clothes drenched; a rivulet of ice-water running down his neck and back; water dripping from his nose and chin; his boots filled with water; up to his ankles in mud; vainly endeavoring to 'keep his powder dry' beneath his wet garments, and you will see in your mind's eye the pickets of the memorable night of the 9th. Many in the trenches and bomb-proofs waked up on the 10th to find themselves in the midst of a sea of water and mud, or half buried beneath a bank of dirt. Tents, breastworks, picket-pits, all caved in. By mutual consent both armies in the morning stopped firing and dragged themselves out of the mud.

Col. Bintliff has returned from Washington but has

been summoned to preside at a court martial con-
vened at Corps Headquarters. Lieut. Col. Pier,
Major Roberts and Captain Hayward are home on
furlough, reveling in the smiles of pretty faces and
the sparkle of loving eyes. Don't think Mr. Editor
that I envy them, for they are brave and gallant men
and have braved death on many a bloody field, and

'None but the brave deserve the fair,'

but I would like a thirty day furlough myself. Captain Kelly is in command of the regiment, and assisted by Capt. Beckwith, Co. G., has strengthened
and fitted up the picket line very much.

Capt. Ballard has returned looking very much as
though he had been where apple-dumplings and
chicken pie abound.

Lt. Nichols, Co. B, is away on court martial at division headquarters. * * * * * * * *

The health of the regiment is good. It drills and
has dress parade just as if we were not constantly in
range of the enemy's muskets and cannon. To-day
Col. Harriman sent the brigade band down to play
'America' to the Johnny rebs. They did not like
it and began to pitch shell at our camps.

Ever yours, £."

From the 17th until the 20th affairs in our immediate front remained remarkbly quiet. Picket firing
was almost entirely done away with, and the opposing
pickets walked and lay exposed to the full view of
each other with perfect impunity. Frequently some
of our men would meet others from the enemy between the lines and trade them coffee for tabacco.
Deserters came over to us in great numbers, and

these little trades were often found to be a convenient means by which these deserters could transmit letters to freinds still in the rebel ranks. All such letters breathed the most unbounded satisfaction of the manner in which the writers had been received and were treated after entering the Union lines, and expressed the utmost regret that they had not come before.

This intercourse could not do otherwise than beget a friendly feeling between those whom the necessities and restraints of the war compelled to be enemies. Conversations, usually of a very amicable character, were frequent between individuals in the opposing lines, though sharp jests and equally sharp retorts were bandied back and forth. "What kind of men are you'uns? it appears to me as though I could whip about five or six like you'uns in fair fight," hallowed a burly rebel across the lines one day. "Braggarts like you are always the first to run when there is real danger," was the curt reply of a Union soldier.

A little incident occurred about this time, that will illustrate the good natured feelings that existed between our boys and the rebels in front. Standing about midway between the lines was a cluster of trees. One cold night, a couple of our adventurous boys, impelled by the discomforts of standing on picket without a fire to warm their benumbed fingers and wet, shivering limbs, determined to visit these trees and secure a supply of wood. Accordingly, taking an axe with them, they proceeded on their errand. Arriving at the trees they immediately commenced operations. The sharp ring of their axe resounded through the night air. "Halloo, Billy!

What are you doing out there?" shouted a rebel picket directly in front and but a few rods distant. "Getting some fire-wood," was the response. "Devilish cold to-night, isn't it?" queried Johnnie. "Yes; how is it with you, plenty of wood?" "Not a stick, and we're almost froze." "Come out here and get some," said our boys. "Hain't any axe," said Johnnie. "Well, you may take ours." "If we go out there will you let us come back?" "O, yes, Johnnie, that is all on the square!" "Well, hurry up, and we'll be over there soon." Our boys provided themselves with an armful of wood for each, and then informed the Johnnies that they could use the axe. Two came over—used the axe until they had secured as much wood as they could carry—returned the axe, and the two parties separated, each wending its way back to its post.

So matters progressed quietly from day to day. But while the infantry was thus quiet on either side, the artillery on both sides indulged daily in furious practice, shelling the opposing lines incessantly for hours together. To protect themselves from the effects of the exploding shells, the men constructed bomb-proofs by digging large square holes, like those dug for cellars to houses, and covering them over compactly with railroad rails taken from the Petersburg and Norfolk railroad, and then covering the rails to the depth of several feet with dirt. Still, even during the most furious shelling, many of the men would neglect to enter the bomb-proofs, so hardy and fearless had they become.

CHAPTER XII.

On the 29th of January, a clear and beautiful Sabbath, about nine o'clock in the morning, a flag of truce was noticed waving above the enemy's works. After waiting a sufficient length of time to be recognized, the bearer advanced to midway between the lines, where it was met by one from our side.

The following letter relates the incidents of the first two meetings of the truce flags, as well as some incidents connected with deserters, and an expedient which the enemy resorted to, to prevent desertions—that of placing their most trustworthy troops as videttes in front of their picket-line, not to guard against a surprise by our forces, but to prevent their own men from deserting; an expedient that, as will be seen, was not always successful.

"Trenches before Petersburg, Jan. 29th.

MESSRS. EDITORS :—A flag of truce, with the necessary excitement accompanying it, has intruded itself upon the monotony of 'life in the trenches,' and the comfort of our winter quarters. We were enjoying (hugely,) all the comforts of our rustic fire-places on a winter's Sunday, when a flag of truce 'came a knockin' at the door.' A trio went down to see what *was* the matter. We found the whole 'Peace Commission,'—no—'Southern Chivalry,' shivering in

G

the wintry wind, and hunting for the right road to the bosom of 'Father Abraham.' One interview with the officer of the picket, resulted in a dispatch requesting an interview with one of Gen. Grant's staff on business of immense importance, and in thirty minutes time. Capt. Burnett, Aid-de-Camp, hastened to lay the matter before the Col. commanding the Brigade, (Col. Harriman,) while Col. Bintliff and myself remained to amuse ourselves with the intense interest and curiosity manifested among the Johnnie rebs.

Soon they came out again, and we went to meet them. Col. Hatch, Asst. Com. of Exchange, came this time, and made known the true state of matters, and said that Vice President Stephens and R. M. T. Hunter were of the party; we proceeded to lay the last communication before Col. Harriman. Soon there was a stir among the natives, and a general spurring to and fro. Col. H. sent Capt. Norton, A. A. G., to division headquarters, and to save time, if possible, rode over to corps headquarters. But, alas for human effort and the waste of horse flesh! the poor 'Peace Commissioners' must stand there for hours, shivering and freezing their toes and fingers, while waiting to be led into the land of promise. They appear to have forgotten that 'large bodies move slow,' and that in the Army of the Potomac everything is 'huge,' and moreover it requires a long pull, a strong pull, and a pull altogether, on the 'colored tape' to move it; and, furthermore, that their villainous treachery, that for four long years has deluged the land in blood and tears, cannot be atoned for in *thirty minutes.*

Gen. Hartranft and Gen. McLaughlin, with their staff officers, have been down, but after waiting till dark for word from City Point, they returned.

Of course, if the Commissioners come over in the morning and proceed to Washington, you will get the news and have a good time and big speeches, and discuss the best manner of dividing the spoils, before this reaches you. But, in the meantime, remember that the rebels have not yet laid down their arms. Soldiers here know that rebel cannon point at us from almost every direction, and rebel works, manned by as brave and tried soldiers as ourselves, frown defiance at us. I believe they are a whipped nation, but the death-struggle has not yet been made. The rebel soldiers themselves have no confidence in the 'Peace Commission.'

Deserters come in rapidly. Three have just now arrived and are being 'picked.' One tall, gaunt, slouched hat, hands-in-his-pocket fellow, in telling of his escape said: 'We're picked men. They've put them on since the 26th. They put us on picket because they thought we'd stick, *but we raised them a bean.*' The manner of the man and the joke was a side-splitter, and we laughed heartily. He says they have often talked of charging our picket line for the purpose of getting bread and meat. A rebel wagon train of forage was charged upon day before yesterday by a brigade, and every vestige of corn taken. They are also very short of clothing.

I'll finish next mail. The health of the regiment is good. We are anxiously looking for Lieut. Col. Pier.

Very Truly, Ɛ."

The ceremonies of the occasion were witnessed by

thousands on each side. Of course no guns were fired on either side—artillery or others—that could by possibility reach near the ground where the flag was received. The affair was deemed of so much moment that it was referred to the President at Washington for instructions, and, of course, considerable delay was occasioned. The 30th was passed away by inquiries and responses. On the 31st at noon, Lieutenant Babcock, of Gen. Grant's Staff, arrived upon the ground to receive the commission. Then a further application was made that Colonel Hatch, the Confederate Commissioner for the Exchange of Prisoners, might be allowed to accompany the Peace Commissioners. This, too, had to be referred to Gen. Grant, and several hours elapsed before an answer was received. At last, just as the sun was sinking behind the western hills, the famous "Peace Commission" was admitted within our lines. An ambulance stood in readiness near fort Morton to convey the Commissioners to Meade's Station, where a special train was waiting to convey them to City Point.

The following letter will be read with interest in this connection:

"Trenches before Petersburg, Jan. 31, 1865.

MESSRS. EDITORS:—This date will be historical. If the poor 'Peace Commission,' which we have just admitted within our lines, fails of its object, from this will date the terribly agonizing death struggles of the bogus confederacy. If it succeeds, this day will be remembered with joy by millions of happy freemen. But from the appearance of this Commission, in my humble opinion they will fail, for

the people of the United States, true to the instincts of a brave and noble people, will submit to no terms —recking nothing of human blood and treasure— but those of justice and humanity.

Correspondence was kept up yesterday between the parties wishing to come in and headquarters. Well dressed and beautiful ladies came down from Petersburg to look at the " detestable Yankees," and in remembrance of home, said Yankees rushed frantically upon the breastworks and heights to get a sight once more of crinoline.

At noon to-day, much to the relief of our suspense, Lt. Babcock, of Gen. Grant's staff, arrived to bid the Commission welcome. Accompanied by the brigade commander, Col. Harriman, and Lieut. Col. Lidig, and Capt. Brackett, of Gen. Willcox's staff, he went out to meet them. This time the Peace Mongers wanted Lieut. Col. Hatch, Asst. Com. of Exchange, to come along with them. Another two, hours were consumed in getting word from Gen. Grant. During this time quite a lively cannonade was kept up to the right of us, reaching near the Commission, probably jogging their memories.

Just as the sun was sinking into a red and smoky horizon, Messrs. Stephens, Hunter, Campbell and Hatch, accompanied by a fine looking negro " boy," passed through an immense crowd of the ragged confederacy, and met between the lines,—on the very ground red with blood of the battle of the 30th of July,—the gallant Yankees who had pushed them into the 'last ditch.' They seemed surprised as they passed along the works at the manifest strength

of our position, and the numbers and fine appearance of our men.

I did not see Vice President Stephens smile, and he looked depressed in spirit. The others were cheerful and light-hearted. Hunter's was the cheerfulness of a bull dog when he *thinks* he's got the bear by the throat. Col. Hatch's cheerfulness was the outgrowth of a kindly heart. Some sharp remarks were dropped by the soldiers as they passed. One 'gentleman from the Emerald Isle' said: '*Be Jazes! if they'd sthaid a month longer they'd not had stringth to come over at all.*'

A 'coach and four' was in readiness to take them to the special train waiting for them, and they filled it and were off, followed by a dashing, galloping troop of general and staff officers.

Their baggage consisted of four dingy looking trunks. It was hurried to the station, and when we had got their baggage safely aboard and bid them God speed and returned to our cheerful blazing hearths, I was too tired and sleepy to finish my letter for the morning mail, so you will have to wait a day.

Some items of interest have transpired lately. Deserters of last night report the breaking of the big dam above Petersburg during the recent rains, washing away the railroad bridge and an immense quantity of government stores. These deserters had no faith in the peace Commission.

Lieut. Col. Pier, of the 38th Wis., has returned, and the boys all gave him as hearty a grip of the hand as ever welcomed back a brave soldier. They are expecting Major Roberts every day.   £."

So the "Peace Commission" went on its useless errand. Every soldier of the Thirty-Eighth, however, will recollect how gladly they saw the Commissioners pass through the lines, and how sanguine the most of the them were that peace was at hand. In fancy they trod the familiar paths of home, and wandered amid the scenes of their native North. Fancy painted scenes where doting fathers and fond mothers should welcome, joyously welcome home, the one long absent "amid dangers' rude alarms.' Then others pictured a place where a warm, wifely bosom would heave with emotions of delight at their coming, and loving arms, should entwine their necks—a wreath more precious than any glory weaves—while little feet pattered their joyous notes of welcome to "papa come home!" And others, still, saw the light of beautiful eyes and sweet, ruby lips— eyes that should beam so tenderly, and lips that should whisper such sweet accents of welcoming praise and trust. Woe to him who just then dared to doubt that the Commission would meet with success. But it came, failed and returned, and the stern realities of war remained after all our blissful anticipations of peace had vanished.

The same routine of duties followed, and the usual mortar and artillery practice was kept up. The weather remained unusually cold—the ground out of the trenches being frozen quite hard.

After the Peace Commission returned, its failure seemed greatly to irritate the enemy. Orders were issued to their pickets to fire upon any of our men showing themselves outside of the trenches. Opposite the Thirty-Eighth, however, these instructions were

never carried out, but on other portions of the line the fire, at times, would be very heavy. The Thirty-Eighth, however, was not allowed to go entirely without some evidence of rebel spleen. No working party, squad or detail could pass into the view of the rebel gunners, but a shell was immediately sent at it. The troops, too, in our front were relieved, and those taking their places, though they did not fire on our Regiment, appeared surly and uncommunicative.

The following extracts from a letter of " F " to the *State Journal* will not be uninteresting:

"Ninth Army Corps, Trenches, }
February 20, 1865. }

MESSRS. EDITORS:—Since the disastrous failure of the late attempt at peace, the rebels in our front have seized every opportunity to vent their spite. Strict orders have been issued to their pickets to fire upon our men whenever seen, and in some instances these orders have been obeyed, the men partaking of the same disappointed spirit. They seem to be especially pitted against the 8th Michigan, one of the regiments of this brigade. 'They never shoot blank cartridges at them.' They have killed and wounded several of the 8th, and a few days since they killed Capt. Robinson, of Col. Cutchin's staff, while he and the Colonel was passing the lines of that regiment. They have also kept up a lively co-tillion with their artillery, which has been vigorously replied to by our guns. At this moment the shot and shell are ploughing the fields and camps, and bursting in the air in the wildest confusion. But I guess, from the way our boys cheer, the rebs are getting the worst of it.

Our mortars plant the shots with great precision right into the forts and into the main line, among their tents, and often penetrating their boom-proofs. Battery E, of thirty-two pounder Rodman guns, is shelling the rebel camps, over two miles away, (easy range for them,) and the terrible missiles drop right into the camps of the astonished enemy. Tit for tat. It is a game they have been playing upon our camps for some time. The rebels have also done well to-day, for they have already put three shot inside the parapet of Fort Morton, and many among the camps. It is what the boys call 'right lively.' Very few of the snobbish gentry would probably believe that a refined and gentle lady, nursed in the lap of luxury, could endure the shock of the cannonade above described. Mrs. Major Eaton was here, and as apparently undisturbed, except for the safety of her liege lord, as if adorning the drawing-room which she seems so well fitted to grace. While she was watching the bursting shells, one mortar shell burst near by, and a heavy fragment struck at the feet of a staff officer, throwing the mud upon him. She considered it quite a curiosity, and took it along when her happy husband and herself left for the North. I would give you the particulars of this romatic 'union under difficulties,' but it would crowd your columns.

Night before last four deserters came through the lines. In the morning, by permission of Col. Harriman, they sent back the following letters:

'United States of America, Feb. 19th 1865.

Mr. G. W. Partridge:

Dear Friend: I seat myself to let you know that

it is all right with us this Sabbath morning. The
Billies treat us mighty well so far. I would have
come a long time ago if I had known how they would
have treated me. ' *You all*' had better come. I
got crackers and sweetened coffee and cheese for my
supper and as much of the 'obejoy' as I wanted.
Things is all right here. We come through saft, and
Blackburn of the 60th is with us, so you may find me
in Hanover, Pa. No more at this time. I hope to see
you all soon, but not in the Confed. I am in a
hurry.   W. L. DAVIS.

      ' Grant's Lines, Feb. 25th, 1865.

We reached here and got plenty to eat and good
whisky to drink. We start for the North free men
again. What you heard is true about the boys that
desert. If you knew what I do you would come to-
night.. This is true. Tell Capt. Reaves I am sorry
for him.   ALFRED WHITTEF,

      Co. F, 59th Ala., Gray's Brig.

P. S.—Please hand this to the 45th Ala.'

Last night four more came in, and to-night the
Capt. Reaves spoken of in the above, came over,
bringing with him a sergeant and corporal. The
captain is a fine looking, proud spirited man, and it
is evident that desertion cuts to his very soul, but he
has seen far more suffering than most of us, and has
been driven to it by despair. He says: ' I have always tried to do about right by the boys, and lead
them bravely and well, but I thought it would be
hardly right to lead them into another fight and have
them butchered up for nothing.'

Col. Bintliff is home on a leave of absence for
twenty days. Col. Pier is in command. The health

of the regiment is good. Convalescents are returning. Capt. Waddington has returned. The boys are feeling good over the glorious news. The question is oft repeated, 'Where in kingdom come *will* the rebs go to now?' F."

CHAPTER XIII.

The continued good news that reached us, of the progress of Sherman northward from Savannah, had a most inspiriting effect on our troops. Desertions from the enemy were both frequent and numerous; and all told tales of hardships and suffering. The following letter will illustrate:

"Head Quarters, First Brigade,
First Div., Ninth A. C., Feb. 25.

During the last two nights twenty-seven deserters have come into the lines of Col. Harriman's brigade fronting the "Crater." They all tell the same story of hardships and suffering; but they bring a piece of intelligence, which, if true, is important. They say the rebels are making every preparation to evacuate Petersburg and fall back on the opposite side of the Appomattox. They also say many are leaving their army to go home to their families and farms. The term of service of Wise's brigade expires on the 1st of March. They say if nothing transpires of a cheering nature before that time they will all go home.

The 'shotted salute,' ordered by Gen. Grant in honor of the capture of Wilmington, was fired this afternoon at 4 o'clock. It created considerable excitement among the rebs. One man of the 51st P. V. V. was killed and one wounded to-day by a shell.

Truly,   £."

Rumors of the kind mentioned in this short letter.
were common in camp, but the discerning minds
easily arrived to the conclusion of their fallacy; for,
by abandoning Petersburg, Lee would have exposed
his entire communications to the mercy of Grant, and
to having his army shut up in Richmond, and it was
hardly to be supposed that so able a leader would
make such a move unless, indeed, he intended to abandon both Petersburg and Richmond and retire to
Danville or Lynchburg.

From this time until the 25th of March, nothing
out of the usual line of occurrences took place.
Picket firing was resumed to some extent during
the night, but between the Thirty-Eighth and the
enemy in front there existed a tacit understanding
that neither should commence firing on the other
without first giving fair warning—an understanding
that was faithfully kept by both parties. The usual
shelling was also steadily kept up, almost daily, and
altogether the position of the Regiment was a warm
one. Day by day the rebels in front grew less communicative. From them we could get little news of
what was transpiring in rebeldom. The trading and
trafficing that had been carried on between the opposing pickets, was prohibited, and comparatively
all intercourse between our men and those of the
enemy ceased.

For several days the Richmond papers had thrown
out suggestions of a contemplated movement by the
rebels. What its nature, character, extent, or the
point to be struck were kept a profound secret.
Only this information was vouchsafed to our anxiously waiting minds: that it would be so startling.

overwhelming and decisive as to surprise the whole world. The wonder transpired at last.

During the fore part of the night of the 24–25th of March, heavy rumbling noises were heard, dogs barked, and many things indicated that a movement of troops was taking place within the rebel lines. Before many hours the movement developed itself. About four o'clock in the morning of the 25th, Lee, having massed his forces during the darkness, behind his lines at the foot of Cemetery Hill, hurled his legions upon Fort Steadman. The careless and negligent picket line of the Fourteenth New York Heavy Artillery, in front of the fort, was surprised and captured without giving any alarm. Over the main line into the fort, the rebel hosts rushed. The surprised troops were shot or bayonetted in their tents, or taken prisoners and sent to the rebel rear. The guns of Fort Steadman were turned upon our own lines, and thus far everything went on swimmingly in the enemy's favor.

The following letter, in the main, gives a correct account of the fight:

" Headquarters First Brigade, First Div., {
Ninth Corps, March 25th, 1865. {

Well, dear *Journal*, Lee *has* astonished the world. At least he has astonished the world of soldiers here in the trenches by a pusillanimous attempt to break the center of our division line, double it upon the flanks, and by following it up, cut our army in two. He would undoubtedly have been successful if he had brought *fighting* men enough along, and if the Ninth Corps had not been on the route.

We were aroused from sleep about half past four

o'clock by desultory shots fired in rapid succession, and a variety of yells from the picket line. Col. Harriman, commanding the brigade, was first in the saddle, and sent his staff officers flying in every direction, carrying orders and ascertaining the state of affairs. The brigade was soon under arms, and ready for any emergency. It was still thought by all to be merely a picket fusilade. But mindful of emergencies, the Colonel ordered me to look at the ground facing Fort Steadman, that he might know where to throw a line of battle if necessary. I obey-ed the order, and emerged from the pines near the Third brigade headquarters. Gen. McLaughlin had just gone down to see what was the matter, accom-panied by his Aid, Lieut. Sturges. I followed for the same purpose. They were both captured, and as I was met by a volley of musketry, I deemed it prudent to retreat in good order, and as fast as my iron gray could carry me. The rebels had turned the Fort Steadman guns upon Fort Haskell, and upon the retreating men of the Third brigade. Their in-fantry were also pressing Fort Haskell, and had ad-vanced a line from the rear of that fort toward Meade's Station, and threatened division headquar-ters, thus isolating our brigade from the division commander. I immediately communicated this to Col. Harriman, who sent two of his regiments—the 37th Wisconsin, and the 109th New York, command-ed by Lt. Col. Pier, of the 38th Wisconsin, to take position at right angles with the main line on the crest of the hill facing the captured fort. The brig-ade pioneers, a heroic little band of men, worked with their might during the entire action, throwing

up a line of breastworks at this point, running at right-angles to our main line, in order to protect the threatened flanks of the brigade.

Gen. Parke, commanding the 9th Corps, and temporarily in command of the Army of the Potomac, sent to know what disposition had been made of the 1st Brigade. Col. Harriman replied that he had thrown two regiments back at right-angles with the main line to protect the flank and shifted his troops well to the right. Gen. Parke returned word that that was right and to keep them in that position until further orders. This proved a drawback to the spirit of the men, who wanted to take a few prisoners from the thousands before them. We might have captured many prisoners, but to charge would leave Fort Morton uncovered, and once in possession of the enemy it would cost us dearly to retake it.

At daylight Gen. Hartranft brought up his (3d) division of new troops at double-quick. They opened a withering fire upon the advanced line of rebels and soon drove them out of the old earthworks behind which they were posted, and occupied them. From these he opened upon the main line. This with the thundering volleys of cannon and musketry from the embrasures and parapet of Fort Haskell on the left, and within thirty rods of them, and Fort McGilvery on the right, within easy range, together with the showers of shot and shell from the forts and batteries surrounding Fort Steadman, made it too warm for the four divisions cooped up in so small a compass. They could also see column after column marching to the support of Gen. Hartranft's line, and a flanking line of breastworks at the only weak point in their

II

front being thrown up and occupied by the right
wing of Col. Harriman's brigade, they now gave it
up as hopeless, and commenced to draw back their
reserves, while the advanced guards kept a bold
front.   Our batteries on the left now aided Fort
Haskell in sweeping the field between the works,
and the scene here was terrible.   The rebels were
mown down in swaths.   Our musketry had told
heavily on them, while hemmed in by the walls of
Fort Steadman, but here we strewed the field with
their dead and dying.   Gen. Hartranft could wait no
longer for orders or reinforcements, but led his division in a brilliant charge.   They came down upon
the frightened rebels like an avalanche.   The 2d
brigade of this division also moved up rapidly on the
right.   At the approach of our men the rebels threw
down their guns by hundreds and surrendered.
Our two divisions made short work of the capture
of two thousand three hundred prisoners.

By nine o'clock A. M. the battle was over and all
was quiet.   Under a flag of truce the rebels asked
for leave to bury their dead, which was granted.

Many of their wounded got back to their lines.
A liberal estimate of their losses in the action will
reach three thousand five hundred.   Among the
captured were three brigade commanders.   We lost
a part of the garrison of Fort Steadman, 250 of the
14th N. Y. Heavy Artillery, and a part of each of the
29th and 57th Mass.   The casualties in our brigade
were five wounded.   Our total loss will probably
foot up between five and six hundred.   Capt.
Swords, of Gen. Willcox's staff, was taken prisoner.
Gen. Deven, commanding one of Gen. Hartranft's

brigades, was wounded. But you will get the particulars by telegraph before this reaches you.

Our troops did splendidly. I have never seen troops in better condition, or more eager to fight since the battle of South Mountain. * * * * *

We have heard nothing definite from attacks on other portions of the line.

A word of regimental matters. The health of the 38th was never better. Quartermaster Rood and Lieut. Pier arrived this morning. Lieut. Col. Pier is in command of the 109th N. Y. V. V. One man of Co. H was wounded in the action by a piece of shell.

Very truly,   £."

CHAPTER XIV.

After the repulse detailed in the previous chapter, the rebels contented themselves with shelling our lines and camps daily, meanwhile keeping closely under cover themselves. Picket firing was resumed, and, especially during the night, was kept up with considerable spirit. Each side became more vigilant, and the rebels less communicative.

About this time, too, some investigations were made into the affairs of the commissary department. For many weeks the enlisted men had complained of the insufficient quantity of rations issued to them, and had been compelled to purchase food to a considerable extent to satisfy the demands of nature. What appeared very singular, and first aroused suspicion that something was wrong was, that the commissary sergeant had considerable quantities of bread and pork to sell. The bread was Government bread, and the pork Government pork. What the investigation evolved has not transpired; but the result was, that Chambers, the commissary sergeant, was reduced to the ranks, and that, from that time, the men received all the rations they needed.

Meanwhile, the grand movement that was to culminate in the fall of Petersburg and Richmond, and the destruction of Lee's veteran army, began. Sher-

idan, after annihilating Early's army, had swept
down from the Shenandoah Valley, and, passing
around to the north of Richmond, destroying roads,
bridges, canals and vast quantities of other property
on his way, had crossed the James River and encamped to the rear of us. The heavy spring rains
had ceased, and the ground was rapidly approaching
a condition to render operations on a large scale
practicable. Five days' rations were kept constantly
in the men's haversacks, all redundant baggage
sent to the rear, and everything made ready to move
at an hour's notice. Troops were continually moving
from the direction of City Point toward the extreme
left. Everything betokened that hot, sharp work
was ahead.

On the 29th, we heard in camp, far off to the left,
the first rattle of musketry. Heavy cannonading occurred at the same time, and gave evidence that the
work had actually begun; and the rumors that
had reached us that the army was again in motion,
were verified. During all this time, until the first
day of April, the Thirty-Eighth laid in the trenches
and watched anxiously the rebels in front, and for
news from the scene of conflict. Wounded and
prisoners in great numbers passed along the rear toward City Point, and gave evidence that work, sharp
and bloody, was being done on the left. But, aside
from the general statement that everything was
going well with our forces, nothing definite reached
us from the scene of conflict.

The first day of April, 1865, was drawing to a
close. All day, at intervals, the sharp rattle of musketry and the thunder of heavy artillery, far on our

left had been heard in camp. We knew that the Second and Fifth Corps, with Sheridan's cavalry, were engaging the enemy. How fared the fight none could tell. The more sanguine, taking counsel from their hopes, believed that our forces had made the most cheering progress, and had succeeded in driving the enemy's right far back; while another class, having just as good means of arriving at a correct conclusion, were just as confident that we were suffering defeat. Nor did the various rumors from the scene of conflict at all tend to relieve the anxiety and uncertainty of these long hours of suspense. One rumor said that Sheridan had reached and cut the South-side railroad, and hurling his impetuous legions on the right flank of the enemy, was rapidly doubling up his right wing; while another story, apparently from just as reliable source, told a tale of hideous disaster—that Warren, with the Fifth Corps, had been driven back, with terrible slaughter, a distance of two miles. Neither of these rumors was wholly true or wholly false. Sheridan, with his cavalry and the Second Corps, had, indeed, made good progress on the left, although he had not yet succeeded in entirely throwing his forces across the South-side railroad, and Warren, by some as yet unexplained combination of events, had been obliged to yield ground to the enemy, and had been relieved of his command by Sheridan.

It was late in the afternoon, and while these rumors were rifest in camp, that I met Col. Bintliff. A few minutes conversation ensued, during which he confidentially informed me that he expected we should have work to do before the next morning. He

said, that, while it was desirable that the men should
be ready to move at a moment's notice, they ought
not to be unnecessarily alarmed, but that it would
be best they should be cautioned that, under present circumstances, we might reasonably expect
an attack from the enemy, or to receive an order to
move, at any moment.

This conversation convinced me that our forces on
the left had gained substantial successes; for, unless
such was the fact, our leaders would never have
dared, with the small force available near our position, to attempt to carry the opposing works in front.
It was only upon the theory that the enemy had been
badly worsted elsewhere, and obliged to materially
weaken his forces at this point, to fill up his shattered
ranks, that the movement would be at all justifiable.

The afternoon was warm and pleasant, and affairs
in our immediate front had been unusually quiet all
day. Only on our right, near the Appomattox river,
and our left from Fort Mahone and its surrounding
batteries, had the enemy that day indulged his pen-
chant for throwing shells. As the evening wore on,
the men gathered in little groups to enjoy its calm
beauty—to talk of home and friends—to sing the
songs that find an answering echo in every soldier's
breast, or to indulge in conjectures concerning the
battle in progress. There are very many of the gallant Thirty-Eighth who will remember how vividly
their hearts gathered around them the sweet influences of home and home scenes, amid the beautiful
lakes and prairies of the North, as the pathetic notes
of "Just before the battle, mother," floated out upon
the quiet evening air. To me it seemed almost as

though the veil that separates the finite from the infinite was drawn aside, and their souls were permitted to catch a glimpse of the future before them, as they sang—

> " Comrades brave are 'round me lying,
> Filled with thoughts of home and God,
> For, well they know that on the morrow,
> Some shall sleep beneath the sod."

As the evening passed away the usual routine of camp duties was strictly observed. At Retreat the men were again cautioned to have everything in readiness to repel an attack of the enemy should one be made, or to move at a moment's notice should it be required. The lights were extinguished, and all was quiet in camp, save the measured tread of the sentinels as they walked their respective beats.

Suddenly, on our right near Fort Steadman, were heard the sharp rattle of musketry and the heavy booming of artillery. What could it mean? Had the enemy attempted a repetition of the affair of the 25th of March? No, it is our men shouting now, while the rebels are still and quiet. It was our forces on the offensive. Soon the rattle of musketry ceased, and only the thunder of cannon was heard. Then the truth flashed upon our minds—our forces had made a feint attack on the rebel works opposite Fort Steadman. Each retired to his quarters, and again all was quiet in camp.

Just after midnight the order was passed to each company commander to call the men into line as stilly and quietly as possible. No lights were made, and, to an observer distant a few rods, nothing unusual in camp would have been perceptible, save perhaps, dark forms flitting noiselessly past in the murky

gloom, like restless spirits keeping their nightly
vigils.

Everything being in readiness, the 51st Pennsylvania was deployed to hold the brigade line, and
our regiment moving by the left flank, marched along
the line past Forts Meikle, Davis and Sedgwick, (the
latter probably better known by the popular name of
"Fort Hell,") just to the left of the latter of which the
regiment was halted, and laid while a brigade of
General Hartranft's Division [the 3d] filed past us.
Here we found the 37th Wisconsin and the 27th
Michigan regiments that had preceded us, and shortly
after the 8th Michigan and 109th New York arrived
upon the ground.

As the last of General Hartranft's Division marched
past, the Thirty-Eighth was ordered to move out and
form in line of battle directly in front of Fort Sedgwick and in the immediate rear of our picket line.
At the same time, the 109th New York, under command of Lieutenant Colonel Pier, and the 8th
Michigan, commanded by Major Doyle, were respectively moved out and formed in line, the former
about ten rods in the rear of the Thirty-Eighth, and
the latter about the same distance in the rear of the
109th New York.

The 37th Wisconsin and 27th Michigan still lay
behind the works to the left of Fort Sedgwick, with
orders, if the assaulting column should carry the fort
in front, to move out immediately, and obliquing to
the right, carry a portion of the enemy's line between
the fort and the Appomattox river.

These dispositions having been made, Col. Harriman, our Brigade Commander, who had retained the

immediate control of matters, and had directed these dispositions of the troops, now sought Col. Bintliff and turned over the command of the assaulting column to that officer.

The responsibilities of the command having thus been thrown upon him at so terribly critical juncture, the intrepid Colonel proceeded to make such arrangements as were possible, in the short space of time that would elapse, before the decisive moment to move would arrive. To Major Roberts he turned over the immediate command of the Thirty-Eighth, at the same time informing him of his reasons for doing so. Hastening to Lieut. Col. Pier and Maj. Doyle, he informed those officers of the cammand to which he had been assigned. " You will lead us, sir, I hope?" said Major Doyle on receiving the information.* Stung by the covert insinuation the chivalrous Colonel sharply replied, "I intend, sir, to accompany my regiment, and I believe it is in advance of yours."

All was ready. Nothing as yet gave any token that the enemy was aware of the terrible visitation that was soon to be upon him. Only a few mortar shells, thrown from a battery to the right of Fort Mahone, and an occasional random gun fired by

* I do not believe that the gallant Major intended any reflection upon the character of Colonel Bintliff. Certanly none could have been more misplaced or uncalled for. Col. Bintliff had been assigned to the command of the Third Brigade, after the capture of Gen. McLaughlin at Fort Steadman, on the 25th of March, but had sought and obtained permission to remain with, and lead his regiment in this action. The curious will, perhaps, find a sufficient key to the Major's meaning in the sudden change of command at so critical a moment, without having the insinuation refer to Colonel Bintliff.

some rebel picket, gave any indication of life within
the rebel lines. But directly in our front, so indis-
tinct that its dim outlines were scarcely traceable
against the western sky, stood the frowning battle-
ments of Fort Mahone, from the embrasures of which,
with those of a dozen surrounding batteries, a withering shower of death was ready to belch forth upon
us with terrible fury.

The appointed moment at length arrived—the signal's flash was seen—and at four o'clock of the morning of the 2d of April, just as the first gray streaks
of dawn appeared in the east, the command was
given, "Column, forward!" Steadily, quietly as it
would had it been on parade, the column moved to
the assault. The trenches of our picket line were
first to be crossed, and down into them sprang the
first line of battle. Here, through some mistake, an
order was given to fire, and instantly the sharp crack
and rattle of musketry rang along the line, and

> " Now, storming fury rose,
> And clamor such as heard on earth till now,
> Was never."

Hardly waiting to reload their guns, the gallant
fellows sprang over the works and on toward the
enemy. The rebel pickets fired one wild, aimless
volley, and fled like frightened deer toward their
main line. "Forward! forward, my hearties!" A
loud, exultant cheer responded from the whole line,
and catching the spirit of the moment, a hundred
voices shouted the inspiring cry, "Forward! forward!" But the enemy is awake now, and fully
realizes the danger that is coming. Every gun he
could bring to bear has been trained upon our column, and rains upon it a storm of death. Above,

and all around, the air is lurid with bursting shells. Solid shot tear wide great gaps of death. Grape and canister shriek through the air as though all the demons of destruction gathered together, were holding high carnival. But above the roar of cannon and the bursting of shells—above the howling of shot, the shriek of canister, and rattle of musketry—above the wail of the wounded, and the groans of the dying, rang out the determined, exultant shout of the Thirty-Eighth. The strong *chevaux de frize* of the enemy was reached, rent apart as though it was a rope of sand, and cast aside. The gallant Kelly sprang forward and fell with a terrible, gaping wound in the side. Forgetful of everything but the mighty issue at stake, the noble fellow raised his head, waved his sword, and shouted, "Forward! For God and our Country, now!" Nothing could withstand the impetuous onset. The *abatis* that surrounded the fort was reached, and the long, sharpened stakes were literally wrenched off or from the ground. The intrepid Wood sprang to the front shouting, "Follow me!" but just as he reached the outer base of the fort, a ball crashed through his left hand and thigh, and he fell to the earth. All the way the ground was strewn with the dead and wounded; but unmindful of loss, and unappalled by any danger, the heroic Thirty-Eighth pressed forward to the work. Nobly emulous of the honor, each strove to be first in the fort. All else seemed forgotten. Officers and privates alike vied with each other in the effort. On, on, with resistless sweep, the line rushed, up the steep slope, over the parapet blazing with fire, down into the works, a short hand-

to-hand conflict, and Fort Mahone, the rebel stronghold, was won.

Immediately the captured guns were manned and
turned upon the enemy. So suddenly had the rebels
been driven from them, that one they had succeeded
in loading remained charged. Our boys rammed
home another, and sent the double charge after the
fleeing enemy. The commandant of the fort was
captured, and his papers secured.

"How do you like the way the Thirty-Eighth performed, to-day?" I asked of Col. Bintliff as we met
and clasped hands a few minutes after. With a look
and a smile that bespoke the highest satisfaction, the
intrepid leader replied, "It was noble; it was glorious! Every man is a hero!"

Having performed the part assigned to us, and the
109th New York and the 8th Michigan having closely followed us into the fort, the 37th Wisconsin and
27th Michigan, following their orders, moved up from
behind the works to the left of Fort Sedgwick, where
they had laid during the storming of Fort Mahone,
and obliquing a little to the right, came into the
works of the enemy just to the right of the captured
fort; but as the enemy had already been nearly, or
quite flanked out of that portion of his line they
were expected to carry, these two regiments were
enabled to get in with a trifling loss.

The gray dawn had whitened into daylight. All
the tools that could be found, suitable for the purpose, had been brought into requisition, and vigorously used to fortify against the counter-assault that
we had every reason to expect the enemy would
make; for, it was idle to suppose that he would re-

sign the lost position, one of such vast importance to
him, without a desperate struggle for its recovery.
Not long had we to wait. The sun was hardly two
hours high in the east, when the enemy was signaled
as being in motion. Every man was immediately on
the alert, and each with alacrity took his allotted
place, and quietly awaited the coming onset.

The bayonets of the enemy were visible as they
moved along behind a line of earthworks that served
them as a cover. In fine style they moved out into
the open field, and, forming at a double-quick,
charged on the works we had taken. Instantly the
whole length of our line belched forth a sheet of
flame. Few ever witnessed so terrible an infantry
fire, while shell, grape and canister swept over the
field like a tornado. Flesh and blood could not stand
up under it, and the broken quivering mass reeled
back and sought safety behind the same cover it had
left but a moment before. Four times, during the
day, the enemy essayed to retake the captured works,
and each time he was repulsed with terrible slaughter. The dead literally lay piled upon each
other. Broken, defeated and disheartened, Gen.
Hill, their leader, slain, the task was abandoned, and
we were left in the quiet possession of the *key to
Petersburg.*

Our success, however, was not achieved without
heavy loss. The Thirty-Eighth went into the action
with less than three hundred men, eighty-four of
whom were placed *hors du combat.* The extent of
the rebel loss can never be ascertained, but it must
have been terribly severe.

In the course of the day, Col. Bintliff was ordered

to immediately assume command of the Third brigade, (McLaughlin's,) and was, therefore, obliged to leave the works for that purpose. Lieut. Col. Pier had, for some time previously, been in command of the 109th New York, and thus the command of the Thirty-Eighth devolved upon Major Roberts.

The gallantry of Col. Bintliff, in this affair shone conspicuously. Previously assigned to a command that would have relieved him from all participation in the dangers of the assault, he sought and obtained permission to remain with his regiment and lead it in the attack. His conduct in the trying position in which he unexpectedly found himself placed, as commander of the assaulting column, showed a coolness, courage and fortitude of the noblest character. To bear a prominent part among a band of officers every one of whom was conspicuous for the gallantry of his bearing, amid dangers the sight of which appalled other troops,* is an honor of which any man may well feel proud.

Lieut. Col. Pier, as above stated, had, for some time previously, been in command of the 109th New York, and led that regiment in the charge. His conduct was such as to win, from both officers and men of that regiment, the heartiest encomiums. It seems singular that, in his report of the operations of this day, Col. Harriman has omitted all mention of Lieut. Col. Pier's name. It can only be accounted

---

*A brigade of troops came into our main line just as the rebels made one of their fiercest charges to recover the captured works. Though the brigade was almost entirely out of danger, the sight so appalled them that officers and men broke and fled.

for on the hypothesis that Col. Harriman was not in a position to witness the conduct of his subordinate officers. Certainly, the unanimous testimony of an entire regiment, officers and men, to the efficiency and bravery of an officer, must have greater weight with any unprejudiced mind, than the omission of that officer's name in the report of a superior, who, having a noble opportunity to win an honorable distinction, avoided the dangers and lost the opportunity, by transferring the post he ought to have filled to another and subordinate officer.

Major Roberts won golden opinions from all by the gallant manner in which he bore himself. A son of Erin gave vent to his admiration by declaring that, "There niver was a bullier boy than that little stub of a Major, at all!"

It would be a pleasant task to recount the various deeds of individual heroism that occurred that day, but that is not within the scope of this work, and it would be unjust to make exceptions, where all behaved in a manner so gallant that they wrung the appellation of "hero" from a commander never profuse of praise.

In this connection, too, must not be forgotten the incident of planting the colors on the enemy's works. The Thirty-Eighth had no colors with it, nor did it have at any time during the campaign. When the regiment left the State, its colors had not been prepared, and so, it was obliged to leave without them, but with the understanding that, as soon as furnished, they should be forwarded to the regiment by the State authorities. From some cause, the colors never

I

reached the regiment while at the front, and were not found until it had returned and encamped near Washington, in April, 1865. Thus, having no colors, the Thirty-Eighth, though acknowledged to have been the first regiment in the fort, was obliged to see the colors of others planted upon it instead of its own. The first colors planted upon the captured fort, were those of the 109th New York, which closely followed our regiment into the enemy's works. The second stand of colors planted on the works, belonged to the 8th Michigan.

I have been thus particular, because a few of the officers of the 27th Michigan, have attempted, through the columns of the New York *Herald* and other newspapers, to claim that honor for their own regiment, and thus rob those to whom it justly belongs.

The fact that, during all the time the fort was being stormed, the 27th Michigan, in pursuance of orders, lay behind our main line of works, which position it did not leave until the fort was captured, ought to be sufficient to settle this question beyond all controversy, and fully dispose of the pretensions of that regiment. But my own observation, perhaps, may not be impertinent here. It was sometime, after, (though how long, I cannot definitely state,) the colors of the 109th New York, and of the 8th Michigan, had been hoisted over the works, that the color bearer of the 27th Michigan came over the parapet into the fort, with the colors of his regiment *still encased.* A Lieut. of our regiment told him to plant the colors on the fort, but he replied, that the Thirty-Eighth had first carried the fort, and were en-

titled to the honor of first planting their colors upon it. Soon after, Major Roberts requested him to hoist his colors, and he did so.

All night the troops lay in the captured works and witnessed the conflagration caused by the cotton and tobacco burnt by the enemy to prevent its falling into our hands, as well as the burning of two rebel gunboats on the Appomattox river, and the stupendous columns of fire that shot heavenward when the fire reached and exploded their magazines.

CHAPTER XV.

About 3 o'clock on the morning of the 3d, the whole line was called up, and every precaution taken to prevent a surprise. As the first gleam of daylight appeared in the east, a strong skirmish line was thrown forward, and the whole line advanced toward the city of Petersburg. As the darkness disappeared, it became evident that no enemy remained to confront us; but that Gen. Lee, taking advantage of the darkness of the previous night, had withdrawn his forces across the Appomattox, carrying with him all the material he could get off with. As it became apparent that the city had been evacuated, less precaution was taken, and the troops pressed eagerly forward, anxious to obtain a sight of the prize for which they had so long and so arduously labored, and risked so much.

But here, as on all other occasions, the good conduct of the Thirty-Eighth shone conspicuously forth. The men, though eager and exultant, and often indulging in ringing cheers, kept from straggling and avoided all rudeness toward the people. A lady, just by whose residence our regiment halted and "rested at will," remarked that she was surprised at the excellent demeanor of our troops. She said that a single regiment of rebel troops would, on entering

the city, make more noise and greater commotion, than did our entire brigade.

Upon arriving in the city, the battalion halted, stacked arms, and rested for a short time. The extravagant joy manifested by the colored population, on our entrance into the city, often led to scenes of the most amusing and laughable description. One instance must serve to illustrate: Just as the regiment entered the suburbs, an old wench was descried across a common, hurrying toward us with all possible speed, in one hand swinging an old sunbonnet, and in her other her apron, and shouting, "Halleluyah! Glory to Jesus, de Linkum sogers am cum!" Hastening up to the column, she would first grasp the hand of a soldier in both her own, and, shaking it earnestly, would turn, hopping and dancing with joy, and throw her arms around some other wench. Her antics soon brought a crowd of "Linkum sogers" around her, drawn there by her voluble and queer expressions. "Oh," said she, "I heerd you 'uns holler yis'day mornin', as me and my ole man lay on de bed, and I tole um I wus dun gone sartin shore de good Lawd would send you 'uns in dis time! I felt dat de good Lawd had heerd my prayer dis time! Oh, I knew de chillen of Jesus was comin', and now here you is!" And then she would indulge in another hand-shaking and hugging scene.

God grant that these poor, oppressed people may not have their hopes of freedom and happiness lost in the mazy labyrinths of "Reconstruction."

After resting a short time, the men were recalled, and the regiment, passing by a circuitous route through a portion of the city, returned to its old

camp in the Union lines. This was rendered necessary, because, when the movement began, none of
the men had taken their haversacks with them, and,
of course, many of them had been without food for
nearly two days. Besides, the men were so worn out
that it was absolutely necessary to allow them a few
hours to rest, before they should be obliged to enter
upon a new field of operations. Tired and worn as
the men were, they could not restrain the expression
of their joy at the great successes that had attended
the Union arms, and bon-fires blazed, powder was
burned, and the jubilation kept up until late at
night.

Many of the contrabands in Petersburg accompanied the forces back to camp. During the siege,
they had acquired a not unnatural dread of shot and
shell, and when they discovered one of the latter
lying on the ground, no matter how harmless its
condition, always gave it a wide berth. Their ex-
citability and nervousness amused the men exceed-
ingly, and many were the jokes perpetrated at poor
Cuffee's expense. Among other methods invented
by the men to give expression to their happiness,
was to sink a hole sufficiently deep to receive a
pork barrel. Planting a canteen of powder, with a
slow-match attached, in the bottom, they would then
place over it barrel, filled with old caps, hats, haversacks, canteens, plates, shoes, and everything available around camp, and touching off the powder,
send the barrel, whirling and scattering its contents
in every direction, hundreds of feet into the air.
Occasionally one would be sent up entirely empty.

One of the latter kind was elevated just after a young darkey had arrived in camp. Hearing the explosion, he turned quickly around and saw the barrel shooting upward. "Oh, Lawd! Oh, Lawd, what's dat?" exclaimed the frightened darkey. "Don't be frightened, Cuffee," said a Lieutenant standing near, "that's the way the Yankees draw water, and they have just sent up a barrel." "Oh, Lawd!" was the only expression the bewildered fellow could utter, in his wonder at a people who placed cannon in the bottom of their wells and shot out barrels of water as they needed them.

On the morning of the 14th of April, preparations were made for a movement. Clothing was packed, tents rolled up, and by 9 o'clock, everything was in readiness to march at a moment's notice. About noon the order came to start, and a few minutes ater the regiment bade a final adieu to the place where, for so many months, it had bravely confronted the enemy, and endured so many privations, hardships and dangers. Passing through Petersburg, we camped that night in the rear of the main line of works constructed by the rebels to the south of the city.

The next day after noon, the regiment started on its march up the South-side Railroad, and camped that night fourteen miles from its starting place. At 3 o'clock next morning it was again on the march, and reached Wilson's Station a little after noon, having made over thirty miles in about twenty-four hours. Compelled to lay in the trenches for months previously, until the men had become unaccustomed

to marching, the journey from Petersburg to Wilson's Station will be regarded as one of extreme severity.

That night we encamped on the plantation of Mr. Northington—tents were put up, pickets established, and everything indicated that our stay there was to be comparatively permanent. The next day, however, the regiment moved about three miles up the road, toward Black and White's. At this place a camp was laid out, and arrangements made to render our stay as comfortable as possible. The usual routine of camp and picket duty was performed, but with the exception of three or four days' work on a fort at Black and White's, the men were relieved from all fatigue duties.

Scouting, at first, was allowed to a great extent, and many were the chickens, turkeys, and quarters of mutton that found their way into our camp; but in a few days, as the inhabitants of the surrounding district came in and took the "Parole oath," it was discontinued, except upon permit from brigade headquarters.

The news of the surrender of Lee's army was received about the 10th, and was hailed with extreme delight. Prisoners, by thousands, passed down toward Petersburg. In every heart there was an all-pervading hope—almost belief—that the long, weary, bloody years of war were finally past, and that the beams of a glorious peace were breaking upon the land.

On the 16th, in the midst of all these rejoicings, came the awful news of the assassination of our good and noble President. The story seemed too

horribly wicked for belief, and, therefore, at first, men were disposed to doubt its truth; but as confirmation of the fact reached us, the idea took possession of the minds of the great mass of the army, that the monstrous crime was but a part of the unnatural and wicked rebellion, and a stern spirit of revenge woke up in almost every heart. Well was it, indeed, for the South that her resistance had ceased; for awful and bloody would have been the penalty exacted of her people.

The day will come, when, with the film of rebellion and hate lifted from their eyes, the people of the South will recognize, in all its noble simplicity, the grandeur of the stainless patriotism of Abraham Lincoln, and proudly claim their share in the priceless legacy his death bequeathed to the American people. Let us rejoice, then, that with our feelings stirred to their uttermost depths, we were saved from meting out a punishment that, after all, could only reach those who were guilty only by association, and those, too, who will yet learn to abhor the crime and its authors, and revere the name of the man who gave his life in his labor for the good of all our people.

Closely following the news of the assassination of the President, came the order for the Ninth Corps to report at Washington. On the 18th it broke camp and marched toward City Point, at which place it arrived on the 20th, about noon. The same afternoon, seven companies embarked on steamers for Alexandria, but three, B, G and K were obliged to remain until next morning. This, however, proved no serious delay to them, as by the superior speed of

the boat in which they finally embarked, they arrived
at their destination within a half hour after the companies that preceded them.

On its arrival at Alexandria, the regiment immediately disembarked and marched to the heights
about two miles back of the city, where it remained
until the morning of the second day, when it moved
to Tennally Town, north of Washington.

CHAPTER XVI.

The camp occupied by the regiment while lying near Tennally Town, was extremely picturesque and beautiful. Surrounded on all sides by a thick growth of timber, a little rill of pure water on the east, and another on the south side, rippling over their pebbly bottoms, while in the distance shone the dome of the National Capitol and splendid country residences dotted the surrounding landscape.

To add to the beauty of the situation, booths and arches of evergreens were erected at Regimental and Company headquarters, and evergreens were planted along the company streets in front of the tents.

While lying here, company and regimental drills were had daily, brigade drill twice a week, and "Dress Parade" every Sunday afternoon. Heavy camp-guards were put out through the day, from which, however, most of the men were relieved at Retreat.

Early in May, the regiment was visited by His Excellency, Gov. Lewis. The regiment was drawn up in line of battle to receive him, and after the customary ceremonies, was formed in double-column by divisions, in close order, after which His Excellency addressed them substantially as follows:

"SOLDIERS OF THE THIRTY-EIGHTH REGIMENT OF WISCONSIN:—It is with feelings of mingled joy and

sadness, that I meet you on this occasion. Joy that, in the dealings of a kind Providence, so goodly a number of you have been spared to us through so many hard fought battles. Joy that you, together with every Wisconsin regiment in the field, have gloriously maintained the honor of our State and country, in the face of the common enemy; and joy beyond measure at the crowning success of the National arms, in this unparalleled struggle with a rebellion greater than has hitherto shook to its foundations any nation; and now that peace is nearly restored, and the authority of the National government vindicated, that you can soon go home to your own firesides and industrial pursuits, where the State of your adoption or nativity, will welcome and honor you. But sadness, because the cruel sods of disloyal Virginia cover the lifeless forms of so many of your brethren, who went forth like you to battle for our country, and whose presence is so much missed in your camp circles—brave, noble men, whose warm hearts beat high with patriotism, and around whose every fibre clustered affection's dearest bands. Sadness and sympathy for your brave, wounded comrades who are ekeing out a miserable death-in-life in our hospitals; and deep sadness also, for the cruel, cruel murder of our loved and honored Chief Magistrate.   *   *   *   *   *   *

Your greatest anxiety, undoubtedly, is to be mustered out and sent home. I have anticipated your desires, and will use every effort in my power to hasten the time of your departure. I had an interview with the Secretary of War a few days since, and he assured me that you shall be sent home at

the earliest possible moment. As soon as he hears from Texas and Arkansas, he will be able to give a definite answer, and he thinks that will be within ten days. I hope you may be on your way home within that time. I want to have you go home as a regiment, and to see you proudly marching through the streets of the Capital city of our own State, and I shall do all I can to secure that result.

I am glad to meet you here as soldiers, and shall be still more happy to meet you at home as citizens, where you will live, honored and respected by your fellow men for the great work you have helped to do, in saving the Nation and preserving our liberties."

At the conclusion of the Governor's remarks, the regiment marched back to its quarters, and His Excellency, accompanied by Colonel Bintliff, returned to Brigade Headquarters. The next morning, at 9 o'clock, he reviewed the entire brigade and expressed himself highly pleased with the fine appearance of the men and the perfection of drill they exhibited. Said an officer who witnessed this review, "This brigade has won a name to be proud of, and it does not lose any of its laurels by close inspection." A day or two after, the Governor paid the regiment another visit, remaining nearly all day, and mingled and conversed freely with the men, who were highly pleased with his affability and the interest he manifested in their welfare.

From this time, until the Grand Review of the "Army of the Potomac and the Ninth Corps" on the 23d of May, little outside of the usual daily routine of drill and camp duties occurred. On the

20th and 21st, however, the regiment took part in the Division Reviews of those days.

On the afternoon of the 22d, the regiment marched from camp to a place a short distance east of the National Capitol, where it bivouaced for the night. The Thirty-Eighth was to be the leading regiment of infantry in the grand pageant, threfore it was necessary for it to be in readiness to move at an early hour the next morning. At daybreak the men were aroused, breakfast was eaten, and the regiment moved into a position so as to be ready to take its place in the column.

What pen can paint the scene of that triumphal day! Washington was a world of flowers, and flags and streamers waved and fluttered in every breeze; and through it all, from 8 A. M. until 4 P. M., flowed a stream down Pennsylvania Avenue, of burnished steel, heaving to the measured cadence of the tread of the victorious legions, and carrying upon its broad bosom, here and there, the glorious banner of our Union. Martial music lent its stirring strains, and beauty smiled, and fair hands decked with choicest flowers the toil-worn victors of the nation. Not when the legions of imperial Rome had returned from their grandest conquests, was there awarded them a day of triumph like this. They might proudly drag a captive people after their victorious chariot wheels, but we, with a loftier pride, could point to our work and say, "Behold, we preserved the life of our nation, and liberty for our enemies."

At the head of the column of infantry moved the Thirty-Eighth. Whether in the cadence of the step,

on the wheel, or in handling arms, the men that day in every act, exhibited the perfection of military movement. Exclamations of "How perfect!" "How splendid!" "Did you ever see anything equal it?" broke, at every step, from the crowd that thronged the street on either side, and every moment the spectators gave expression to their admiration by cheers and clapping of hands.

It was a proud day for our soldiers. Their great work was done, and this was to be its brilliant and fitting close.

After passing the reviewing stand, on which sat the President, Gen. Grant, the Secretaries of the various Departments, the Foreign Ministers and other notables, the regiment moved into one of the by-streets, where the men were allowed to rest for a short time, and then we moved back to camp.

In a day or two an order was issued to muster out all men, in the Ninth Corps, whose term of enlistment would expire before the first day of October. This reached nearly all in companies G, H, I, K, and considerable numbers in the other companies. On the 2d of June, all those of the regiment entitled to it, were mustered for discharge. Those of the four companies so mustered, who were not entitled to be discharged, were transferred to other companies.

With the break of day on the 6th, those who were to be discharged, took leave of their less fortunate comrades, and marched to the depot of the Baltimore and Washington Railroad. Col. Bintliff, Maj. Roberts and several other officers of the regiment, accompanied the detachment to the cars. Lieut.

K

Col. Pier, who was at the time in Washington, serving on a court martial, met it at the depot. After waiting several hours, the detachment went aboard the cars, and bidding their last "soldier's good-bye" to those who had accompanied them from camp, started for home.

That night the detachment reached Baltimore, and immediately marched to the depot of the Pennsylvania Railroad, where a train was waiting to receive it. At Pittsburg an excellent breakfast was furnished to the detachment, at the Soldier's Rest, on the morning of the 9th. The next evening it reached Cleveland, and received the generous and really magnificent hospitalities of the people of that city. The change from the cars to steamer here, proved an agreeable relief from the monotony of railroad traveling, and enabled the men to secure the luxury of a night's good sleep. Arriving next morning at Detroit, an excellent breakfast was furnished by the citizens, to which the men did ample justice. Immediately after breakfast, the detachment went aboard the cars and started for Grand Haven. At Owasso, a little station on the road, the people of the surrounding country had gathered in, and furnished us with a bountiful repast. This manifestation of good will on the part of the people of our sister State, unexpected on our part, as it was generous on that of our entertainers, will be remembered with gratitude as one of the brightest episodes in our lives.

The next evening the detachment reached Grand Haven, and immediately went aboard the boat for Milwaukee. The trip, from Grand Haven to Milwau-

kee, will be remembered as the most dreary and uncomfortable part of our journey home. Even the slow time, on platform cars, from Washington to Baltimore, was a luxury, compared to the crowded condition of the men, and offensive and insolent conduct of the officials and employes of this boat. The broad contrast between the demeanor of these men and that of the gentlemanly and obliging officers and employes of the boat that carried us from Cleveland to Detroit, grated most harshly upon our feelings.

We arrived at day-break in Milwaukee. Our reception by the people was not merely generous—it was sumptuously elegant. Everything that could tempt the palate of a hungry soldier, was spread upon the tables with lavish profusion, while the beauty, worth, and social excellence of the city, gave hands, unused to toil, to the willing task of serving the "boys coming home."

On the evening of the same day, June 11th, the detachment reached Madison, when the usual kind of meal, furnished to all of our returning soldiers, was served to them. The next morning, with detachments from three other regiments, amid the thunder of cannon and ringing of bells, it marched from Camp Randall to the Capitol Park, where it was addressed by Gen. Fairchild, Secretary of State; Major Keyes, and several other gentlemen. After giving rounds of cheers for the Union, for Wisconsin and her Governor, the troops marched back to camp, and this closed, substantially, their career as soldiers in the Great Army of the Union. On the 20th, the men were paid off and finally discharged.

CHAPTER XVII.

It was expected when the first detachment of the regiment was mustered out, that the remaining portion would be consolidated with the 37th Wisconsin, but the order for that purpose was never carried into effect. The regiment remained quietly in its camp, doing such duties as were required of it.

During its stay here, Col. Bintliff resigned, and was mustered out on the 26th of June, the command devolving upon Lt. Col. Pier, who was soon after commissioned as Colonel. On the 1st of July, Major Roberts was mustered out, and shortly after Capt. Ballard of company A, was commissioned as Lieut. Colonel, and Capt. Hayward, of company B, as Major. Owing, however, to the paucity of numbers in the battalion, none of these officers were able to muster under their commissions.

On the 25th of July, the battalion was mustered for discharge. The men had waited impatiently for this time, and the delay had proved extremely irksome to their anxious spirits; but as the prospect of again seeing home and friends brightened, the brave fellows gave vent to their unbounded joy.

It would be useless to attempt to describe their journey home, as, in its main features, it was but a repetition of the experience of the first battalion,

already described. Everywhere along the route, they were greeted with cheers and the waving of flags, handkerchiefs and hats. A grateful people joyfully welcomed them home from the scenes of their toils, dangers and victories.

The reception of the battalion at Madison was the same as that extended to the first,—Gov. Lewis, who had returned from visiting our sick and wounded soldiers in southern Hospitals, Gen. Fairchild and others, making addresses, welcoming the soldiers home. Col. Pier responded in a short speech, in which he recounted the deeds the regiment had performed,—eulogized the bravery, patience, fortitude and other high soldierly qualities of the men, and concluded with the prediction that, in the retirement and walks of civil life, they would prove themselves good and worthy citizens, as they had already proved themselves brave and excellent soldiers.

After the ceremonies of the reception had ended, the detachment marched back to camp. On the 15th of August, 1865, the men were finally paid off and discharged; and the name, and the deeds, and heroism of the gallant Thirty-Eighth Regiment passed into history, and became the legacy of as brave and noble a band of men as ever battled for Liberty and against Wrong, to the people of our State and of the Nation. So long as they shall esteem courage and despise baseness—love patriotism and detest treason—so long will the memory of its deeds and its sacrifices be cherished in the grateful hearts of those whose liberties it helped to preserve.

BIOGRAPHICAL

SKETCHES.

BIOGRAPHICAL SKETCHES.

FIELD AND STAFF.

7429 Bond av
Chicago

COL. JAMES BINTLIFF.

The subject of this sketch was born in the county of York, England, on the first day of November, 1824, and, therefore, was in his fortieth year when he took command of the Thirty-Eighth Regiment of Wisconsin Infantry. In his personal appearance, Colonel Bintliff is above the average of men. Standing fully six feet high, a forehead full and of more than medium breadth and height,—a bluish gray eye,—a long nose, deviating slightly from straight—firm set lips, and a chin neither prominent nor retreating, the whole features surmounted by a thin head of lightish-brown hair, and you have a picture of Colonel Bintliff. In his carriage he is usually inclined to stoop; but when once aroused or excited, his posture becomes erect and dignified.

In the spring of 1842, he came to the United States, and settled in central New York, where he resided until the fall of 1851. In November of that year, he removed to Wisconsin and settled in Green county, where he continues to reside.

In August, 1862, he raised a company for the 22nd regiment, and was elected and commissioned its Captain, and mustered into the United States' service on the 2d of September of that year. On the 16th of the same month his regiment left the State to report to General Lew Wallace, then in command at Cincinnati, and he accompanied it. The city was at that time threatened by a strong force under command of the rebel General Kirby Smith, who had approached within three miles of it.

Upon reporting to General Wallace, the regiment was assigned to a position on Covington Heights, and thus became a part of the army of Kentucky. The movement of Kirby Smith was designed to cover the concentration of supplies for the rebel army, which had, for some time previously, been going forward at Camp Dick Robinson, Ky., and to facilitate their removal, as well as to co-operate with the army of General Bragg, which was then invading Kentucky. The failure of Buell to fight Bragg at Perrysville, neutralized all the operations of our armies in the West during that year, and enabled the rebels to escape with their accumulated plunder into East Tennessee.

In February, 1863, the Army of Kentucky, of which the 22d regiment was a part, numbering twenty thousand men, under the command of Gen. Gordon Granger, marched from Danville, in that State, to Louisville, where it embarked on steamers, and under a convoy of gunboats, went, via the Ohio and Cumberland rivers to Nashville, Tennessee, and became the Reserve Army of the Cumber-

land, its position being on the extreme right and extending to Franklin.

On the 4th of March, 1863, the brigade to which the 22nd Wisconsin was attached, with one battery of artillery, under the command of Colonel John Coburn, of the 23d Indiana, (who is maliciously suspected of having been in search of a Star,) moved out from Franklin to the front, in the direction of Thompson's Station. On the 5th, Coburn engaged the enemy 15,000 strong, under the command of Van Dorn. The engagement commenced at 10 o'clock in the forenoon, and continued with great obstinacy until 3 P. M. The brigade was annihilated. About 700 men were killed or wounded, and 1,700 taken prisoners.. Only 300 or 400 escaped. Capt. Bintliff was one of the few, who, at the last moment, made their escape.

The fragment of his regiment was sent to the rear, half way between Franklin and Nashville, to guard the railroad depot at Brentwood. On the 25th of the same month, Gen. Forrest, who, with two brigales of cavalry had succeeded in passing around the extreme right of Gen. Rosecrans' line, at Franklin, and in gaining the rear of his line, surrounded the camp at Brentwood before daybreak, and before the garrison was aware of his approach. After a feeble resistance the entire command was captured, and before 7 A. M., on its way to Richmond and Libby Prison, where it arrived on the 9th of April.

On the 6th of May, Capt. Bintliff and his fellow prisoners were exchanged at City Point, and sent to Annapolis. Arriving at the latter place, they were

at once ordered to report at St. Louis for reorganization. In June they were again sent to Tennessee, and stationed at Franklin and Murfreesboro.

In January, 1864, he resigned his commission to accept the appointment of Commissioner of the Board of Enrollment, which had been tendered him by the President. On the 8th of March following, he was commissioned by Gov. Lewis, Colonel of the Thirty-Eighth Regiment of Wisconsin Volunteer Infantry, and immediately gave all his energies to raising and filling up the ranks of his command. Owing to a variety of causes enumerated in the first chapter of this work, it was not until after the middle of the next September, that the ranks of the regiment was filled, and the command ready to take the field.

On arriving at the front and merging the two battalions, he immediately commenced the work of discipline and instruction, in which the men were sadly deficient. The new companies because too recently enlisted, and the old ones because the overburdening duties theretofore required of them, had allowed no time for instruction.

At the battle of Hatcher's Run, on the 27th of October, Col. Bintliff handled his regiment with skill and coolness.

For several weeks, during the winter, following he was in the command of the brigade, and in this position, as in others, commanded the respect and esteem of all. His gallantry and daring on the 2d of April, 1865, at the storming of Fort Mahone, was conspicuous, and won for him the confidence and admiration of all those whose fortune it was to witness it. He had been previously assigned to the

command of the 3d brigade of the division to which
he belonged, but suspecting that his regiment was to
take part in the approaching fight, sought, and
obtained permission to remain with it and lead it.
The manner in which the command of the entire assaulting column was unexpectedly throw upon him,
has been detailed in a previous portion of this work.
After the capture of Fort Mahone, Col. Bintliff was
ordered out of it and to the command of the 3d brigade, which position he held during the march up
the South-side railroad to Wilson's station, and until
after the Corps arrived at Washington.

Col. Bintliff was a strict disciplinarian, and made
little allowance for the idiosyncrasies of men trained
in a sphere of the utmost freedom of thought, speech
and action, and hence, his measures often had an appearance of stern and unnecessary harshness. His
first requirement of his soldiers was implicit, un-
questioning obedience, and woe to him who failed of
these. On the other hand, no commander could
move quicker than would he to right any wrong
when once convinced that any of his men were suffering it.

Of an excitable temperament, he was often hasty,
and even boisterous, in his manner, indulging in
language to his men, which he, more than any other,
would regret when his passion had passed away;
but in the hour of danger he was always himself
cool and collected.

Col. Bintliff was promoted to Brevet Brigadier
General of U. S. Volunteers, for, as the order says,
"conspicuous gallantry at the assault on Petersburg,
to date from April 2d, 1865." As very few Brevets

were conferred for that reason, this promotion will, of course be more highly prized. Gen. Bintliff was honorably discharged from service, June 26th, 1865.

———

LIEUT. COL. COLWERT K. PIER.

Lieut. Col. Colwert K. Pier was born at Fond du Lac, in the then Territory of Wisconsin, on the 7th of June, 1841, and was, consequently, only in his twenty-third year when commissioned Lieut. Colonel of the Thirty-Eighth Regiment. His father moved to Wisconsin in 1836, and is the oldest resident of Fond du Lac county. It was there that the subject of our sketch, when Indians were numerous, and with Indian children for playmates, passed the days of his boyhood, attending a district school, or performing such labors as were usual for a boy of his age, whose parents resided on a farm in a new country.

At the age of sixteen he was sent to Lombard University, Galesburg, Ill., where he finished his education, so far as the schools were concerned. In 1860, he commenced to read law in the office of the Hon. Robert Flint, of Fond du Lac.

Upon the call of the President, in April, 1861, he, it is supposed, was the first man in Fond du Lac county to respond, enlisting as a private in the 1st Wisconsin Regiment, and campaigned it with that organization, carrying a musket for three months, in Virginia.

The following autumn, he attended a course of law lectures at the Albany Law School, New York.

Returning to Wisconsin, he took an active part, in 1863, in organizing the State Militia, and was successively commissioned as Captain of Zouaves and Colonel of the 2nd Regiment of State Militia. During this time, also, he was in a law office in Fond du Lac.

In March, 1864, he was commissioned Lieutenant Colonel of the Thirty-Eighth Regiment, and in May left the State in command of the First Battalion, and was present with it in all its marches and battles up to its consolidation with the Second Battalion, at Poplar Spring Church, on the 30th of September, 1864. In the battle of the 17th of June, for the possession of the Norfolk railroad, he was slightly wounded. From the 30th of September, 1864, until early in March, 1865, Colonel Pier remained with the regiment, except while home on a short leave of absence, accompanying it to Hatcher's Run, on the 27th of October, and in all its subsequent movements.

About the 1st of March, 1865, he was assigned to the command of the 109th Regiment of New York Veteran Volunteers, and took part in the operations of our forces in retaking Fort Steadman from the rebels, on the 25th of that month. His conduct, on this occasion, was such as to inspire the men under his command, with the fullest confidence in his coolness and steady courage. On the 2nd of April, he gallantly led that regiment in the assault on Fort Mahone, and by his influence, did much to inspire the men with the steadiness and bravery they showed that day.

During the march up the South side railroad and

back, and the voyage to Washington, he still remained in command. Shortly after the arrival of the Brigade at Tennally Town, he was relieved of the command of the regiment, and subsequently detailed on duty, as a member of the Division Court Martial sitting at that time in Washington.

On the discharge of Brevet Brig. Gen. Bintliff, Colonel Pier was commissioned Colonel of the Thirty-Eighth, but owing to the regiment's not numbering sufficient men, he was unable to muster.

Colonel Pier has a fine personal appearance and an engaging address. Is about five feet nine or ten inches in height, and has a fine head of brown hair, a broad and rather high forehead, blue eyes, a prominent and slightly Roman nose, thin lips, rather full chin, and light complexion. He is sociable, generous and companionable, quick and decisive, yet seems to lack that perfect steadiness that is necessary to insure the highest state of discipline in a command.

MAJOR C. P. LARKIN.

Was born in the city of Milwaukee, Wis., on the 12th day of April, 1844, and was, therefore not quite twenty years of age when commissioned Major of the Thirty-Eighth Regiment. His father is Charles H. Larkin of Milwaukee, and, if we mistake not, at one time sheriff of the county of that name. The boyhood of Major Larkin was passed at school, in acquiring an education. At one time he attended the State University at Madison, and subsequently the Alfred University, Allegany county, N. Y.

Upon leaving the University, he entered the law office of the Hon. Levi J. Hubbell, and began a course of reading in order to fit himself for the practice of the law.

When the 24th regiment was organized, he was commissioned as Second Lieutenant of company H. He accompanied the regiment when it left the State, and was with it at the battle of Perryville. Sometime afterwards, in consequence of sickness, he resigned and returned home. Recovering his health he assisted in raising company B, First Wisconsin Heavy Artillery, and was commissioned its Junior First Lieutenant. On the 17th of March, 1864, he was promoted to Major of the Thirty-Eighth Regiment, and left the State with the First Battalion, under the command of Lieut. Col. Pier. He took part with the battalion, in the battle on the Norfolk railroad, June 17th, 1864, and was severely wounded by a musket ball which entered his left side, between the ribs and hip, and lodged internally, where it still remains. In consequence of this wound he was honorably discharged, from the Military Service of the United States, on the 2d of September, 1864.

Major Larkin now resides in Milwaukee, and is engaged in the practice of his profession. He is six feet in height, has a light complexion, brown hair, and gray eyes.

L

MAJOR R. N. ROBERTS.

Was born in the kingdom of England, on the 30th day of August, 1841, and was, therefore, in his twenty-third year at the time he entered the Military Service. His father was a merchant, and young Roberts passed his boyhood in attending school. When he was two years old, his father removed from England to the United States, and settled in Wisconsin.

On the 15th of April, 1864, he was commissioned Captain of company B, Thirty-Eighth Regiment, and left the State with his company when the First Battalion went. He was with his company in all its marches, and took part in all its battles in which it was engaged. After Major Larkin was discharged, he was promoted to Major, his commission bearing date September 27th, 1864. From the time of his promotion, he remained constantly with the Regiment, except during a short leave of absence the next winter.

At the assault and capture of Fort Mahone, on the 2d of April, 1865, he commanded the Regiment, and behaved with great intrepidity and daring. He remained in command during all the subsequent movements of the Regiment until after it reached Washington.

Major Roberts is short of stature, being only five feet, three and a half inches in height, but is stout and robust. He has a dark complexion, brown hair and brown eyes, and is social, genial and fond of company and conviviality.

Captain Anson Rood was born in the town of Jericho, Chittenden county, Vermont, on the 23d day of September, 1827. In 1837, his father removed his family to Chicago, Illinois, and the next year to Joliet, in the same State. In 1841, his father and himself went into the Wisconsin Pineries, penetrating to the Eau Claire river, in what is now Marathon county, and were the first white settlers on that stream. In 1842, the family removed from Joliet to Madison, Wis., and there the subject of this sketch made his home until his marriage, on the 10th of February, to Miss Clara A. Sylvester. Shortly after this he removed to Stevens' Point, in Portage county, and engaged in mercantile business. While residing at that place, he was elected a member of the City Council, and its President. He also represented his district, one term, in the State Legislature. He subsequently removed to Adams county, settling in the town of Dell Prairie. In 1863, he was elected to represent that county in the State Legislature, and performed his duties in a manner that was creditable to himself and to his constituents.

In April, 1864, he was commissioned as Quartermaster of the Thirty-Eighth Regiment of Wisconsin Volunteers, with the rank of First Lieutenant. In August following, he was detailed to take charge of the recruiting service for the regiment, and by his energy and tact, materially assisted to fill its ranks.

When the Second Battalion went to the front, he accompanied it, and on its arrival in Virginia, assumed the full duties of the Quartermaster's Department. His administration of the affairs of his office proved very successful, and he was therefore advanced in rank, receiving a commission, dated February 9th, 1863, from President Lincoln, as Assistant Quartermaster of United States Volunteers, with rank of Captain. But having become strongly attached to the Thirty-Eighth, he deferred mustering under his commission, for fear he might be compelled to separate from the regiment, until after it had reached Washington. On the 26th of May, however, he assumed charge of the Quartermaster's Department of the First Brigade of the First Division of the Ninth Corps.

Captain Rood has a fine personal appearance, being six feet in height and well proportioned, and strikes an observer at once, as being a shrewd, intelligent, energetic Western man.

H. L. BUTTERFIELD, REGIMENTAL SURGEON.

H. S. Butterfield is a native of Cheshire county, New Hampshire, and studied medicine in Monroe county, New York, with Dr. Lucius Clark, now of Rockford, Illinois. He subsequently attended medical lectures at Geneva, New York, and afterwards entered Willoughby College, at which he graduated in 1845. In 1864, he removed to Wisconsin, and settled at Waupun, and began the practice of his profession.

In 1856, he served one term in the State Legislature. On the 11th of March, 1864, was commissioned Surgeon of the Thirty-Eighth Regiment, and accompanied the First Battalion to Washington, White House Landing, Cold Harbor, and to the front of Petersburg. During all this time, he performed his duties in a manner to secure the respect and esteem of the men of the regiment. We never heard a member of the Thirty-Eighth speak otherwise than to his credit when referring to him.

Surgeon Butterfield returned home with the last detachment of the Thirty-Eighth, and was honorably discharged from service, August 11th, 1865.

HUGH RUSSELL, FIRST ASST. SURGEON,

Of the Thirty-Eighth Regiment of Wis. Vol. Inft'y, was born in Down county, Ireland, on the 7th of August, 1827. In 1849, he emigrated from Ireland, and came to the United States, settling in Chatauque county, in the State of New York, where he remained for about a year. He then removed to Wisconsin, and settled in Fox Lake, Dodge county.

Previously to leaving Ireland, he comenced the study of medicine at Belfast. After arriving in this country and settling in Wisconsin, he pursued his studies at Rush Medical College, Chicago, Illinois, and graduated at that Institution in the spring of 1854. He then returned to Fox Lake and immediately began the practice of his profession in which he was fairly successful.

On the 5th of March, 1864, he entered the Military Service of the United States as First Asst. Surgeon of the Thirty-Eighth Regiment of Wisconsin Infantry,

with the rank of First Lieutenant.   He accompanied
the First Battalion when it left the State, and did
all that a faithful officer could do, to alleviate the
sufferings of the sick and wounded men of the command.

Surgeon Russell is about five feet ten inches high
has a fair complexion, brown hair and blue eyes.   He
is somewhat eccentric, abrupt and brusque in his
manners, hasty and impetuous in his temper, but is
generous to a fault, and possessed of quick, warm
sympathies that are deeply moved at the sight of suffering.   There were few officers in the Regiment at
the close of its service who had more warm friends
among the rank and file, than did Surgeon Russell.
He was honorably discharged from service, July
5th, 1865.

SURGEON C. B. PIERSON.

We are unable from want of data, to furnish anything approximating a biographical sketch of this individual.   Surgeon Pearson, we believe, is a native
of New England, and is about fifty years of age.   He
was commissioned as Second Asst. Surgeon of the
Thirty-Eighth Regiment in the spring of 1864, and
during the summer had charge of the examination of
recruits for that Regiment, as well as the care of the
health of that portion of it remaining at Camp Randall.

When the last battalion left the State for the seat
of War, Surgeon Pearson accompanied it, and remained with it until sometime in November, when he
resigned and returned to the State.   He is quiet, dignified and gentlemanly in his deportment.

C. TOCHTERMAN, SECOND ASST. SURGEON.

He was born in Switerland, October 30th, 1826, and received a liberal education, graduating at the University at Berne.

In the spring of 1852, he emigrated from his native country and came to the United States. On his arrival in this country, he first settled in the State of Illinois, where he lived about four years, and then removed to Green county, Wisconsin, where he has resided ever since.

August 7th, 1862, he enlisted as a private in company G, of the 22d Regiment of Wis. Vols., and served successively as a common soldier, nurse in hospital, Dispensing Clerk and Hospital Steward.

He was taken prisoner of war on the 25th of March, 1862, and sent to Libby Prison, Richmond, Va., and there paroled. In June following, he was exchanged and returned to duty. Accompanied Sherman's army in its great march from Look-out Valley to the Sea, during which time he was detailed in the Field Hospital, as attendant at the amputation table.

November 29th, 1864, he was commissioned as Second Asst. Surgeon of the Thirty-Eighth Regiment, with the rank of First Lieutenant. On the 31st of January, 1865, he reported for duty in this Regiment, and remained with it during all its subsequent operations and movements, until it was finally mustered out.

Surgeon Tochterman is a fair specimen of the men of his native country—is strong and robust of con-

stitution—shrewd and cautious—anxious to perform his duties conscientiously and well, and is a quiet and worthy citizen.

— *J.S Dearborn* C.

LIEUT. AARON H. McCRACKEN, ADJUTANT.

Aaron H. McCracken, Lieutenant and Adjutant of the Thirty-Eighth Regiment, was born near the village of Monroe, Green county, Wis., on the 14th day of February, 1839. His boyhood was passed upon his father's farm, until he was thirteen years old, when he began a two-years apprenticeship in the drug store of J. K. Eilert, in Monroe. At the expiration of his apprenticeship, he alternately taught and attended school, until his twentieth year, when he entered the State University, Madison, Wis. Here he remained, attending to his studies, until the 11th of August, 1862, at which time he left the Junior Class of that Institution, and enlisted as a private in company G, of the 22d Regiment of Wisconsin Volunteers. In this company he successively served as private, Corporal and Sergeant, until the 3d of May, 1864, when he received a commission as Lieutenant and Adjutant of the Thirty-Eighth Regiment. He reported at Madison, and was mustered into service under his commission in nine days thereafter.

When the First Battalion left the State, Adjutant McCracken remained to assist in recruiting.

On the 22d, when the Second Battalion left the State, he accompanied it, and remained with the regiment nearly all the time until it was mustered out. He was present during the affair at Hatcher's

Run, on the 27th of October, 1864, and took part in the assault at Fort Mahone, April 2d, 1865.

In person, Adjutant McCraken is rather slight, but well knit, and capable of great endurance, when it is required. He was a faithful officer and performed the duties of his position in a most satisfactory manner. He took great pride in the appearance of the Regiment, and it was no fault of his if it failed to rank at the head in that respect.

J. M. WALKER, CHAPLAIN.

J. M. Walker was born in the State of Pennsylvania, on the 23d day of January, 1823. His parents, however, resided, both before and after his birth, in what is now the State of West Virginia.

In early life, he enjoyed good educational advantages. At the age of fourteen, he entered Wellsburg Academy, at which Institution he remained four years. Upon leaving that Institution, he went into business; but, being passionately fond of the law, he at the same time began a course of study and reading to fit himself for the legal profession.

At the age of nineteen or twenty, occurred that which, however, was to change his entire course. In answer, as he believes, to the prayers of a pious mother, the Lord inclined his heart to seek for mercy at the Throne of Grace, and he was made happy in a saving knowledge of the Truth. Following his inclinations, he connected himself with the Methodist Episcopal church.

In 1845, he was admitted as a member of the Rock River Annual Conference, which, at that

time, embraced within its boundaries the north half of the State of Illinois, and all the region of territory lying to the north and northwest. His appointments have always been, however, within the limits of what is now the Wisconsin Conference.

Among the more prominent of his pastoral charges are, Beloit, Whitewater, Beaver Dam, Milwaukee, (Spring Street Church,) Waukesha and Waupun. He also served four years as Presiding Elder of Beaver Dam District, and left a highly prosperous charge to his successor.

When the war broke out, he labored assiduously to promote volunteering. Determining at last to go himself, anyway, he, in August, 1864, enlisted in the Thirty-Eighth Regiment. On the 20th of September, he was commissioned and mustered as Chaplain of the Regiment, and two days after, accompanied the Second Battalion to Virginia, and afterwards accompanied and remained with the regiment until the last detachment was mustered out and sent home.

Chaplain Walker is a good and interesting speaker, short, robust, and always possessed of a happy and contented spirit.

OFFICERS OF THE LINE.

COMPANY A.

CAPTAIN CHARLES T. CARPENTER.

Charles T. Carpenter was born at Ithica, Tompkins county, N. Y. His father was a farmer, and Charles remained at home until he arrived at his majority. Toward his parents and sisters he always exhibited the warmest filial affection. He was ever a modest boy, and as his years increased his diffidence grew upon him.

On arriving at twenty-one years of age, he learned the carpenter and joiners' trade, and followed it as his business until 1856. That year he came to Wisconsin, and entered the store of his brother at Fond du Lac, who had preceded him several years. Here his manly bearing, gentlemanly deportment and strict integrity, won for him the respect and esteem of the community, and drew around him a large circle of friends.

In 1861, he promptly responded to the call of the President for troops, serving as an enlisted man with the First Wisconsin Infantry, during their services as a three months regiment.

As a soldier he was ever ready and prompt in the discharge of duty. By exposure and over-exertion, during this time, he brought on an attack of typhoid

fever, and for weeks his mind wandered and he hung on the verge of eternity.

Having recovered his health, he returned to Fond du Lac, and established himself in Mercantile business. While thus engaged he was elected First Lieutenant, and subsequently Captain of Zouaves.

When the Thirty-Eighth was called for, he immediately began the work of raising men for it, and in April, 1864, was commissioned Captain of company A. When the First Battalion left the State, he accompanied it. Always ready for duty, gentlemanly and kind, he won the respect and esteem of all with whom he associated.

During the battle of the 17th of June, on the Norfolk railroad, he led his company in a most gallant manner. After the Battalion fell back from the first charge, leaving Major Larkin lying severely wounded on the field, Capt. Carpenter was the first to generously spring forward to the Major's rescue, and brought him off the field.

The next day, during the assault on the enemy's line, the Captain was severely wounded in the hand by a minnie ball. This, with a physical system much reduced in vigor, compelled him to leave his command a few days after. He subsequently obtained a Sick Leave of Absence, and returned to his father's in Ithica, N. Y., where he died on the 3d of September following, surrounded by his relations and friends. But though dead to earth, in the memories of his brother soldiers and the community in which he resided, he "still lives."

CAPTAIN C. L. BALLARD.

Captain C. L. Ballard was born in Machias, New York, on September 26th, 1839. In the summer of 1856, he removed to Wisconsin, and settled in Milwaukee, following the business, if we mistake not, of gas-fitter.

On the 5th day of September, 1861, he volunteered as a private in company D, First Wisconsin Volunteer Infantry. On the 8th of October following, he was promoted to Corporal. On the 28th of the same month, the regiment left the State and proceeded to Louisville, Ky. He took part with his regiment in the battle of Mumfordsville, Ky., December 16th, 1861, and Perryville, October 8th, of the same year, and was on that day promoted to Sergeant. He remained with the regiment, and subsequently took part in the battles of Jefferson's Pike, Stone River and Hoover's Gap, in Tennessee, Dug Gap and Chickamauga, in Georgia; Look-out Mountain and Mission Ridge, Tennessee, and Buzzard's Roost, Georgia.

On the 1st of April, 1854, he was promoted to First Lieutenant of company A, of the Thirty-Eighth Regiment, and reported and was mustered in on the 30th of the same month.

When the First Battalion left the State, he accompanied it, and took part in the battles in which the Battalion engaged. At the Battle of the Mined Fort, July 30th, 1864, he was the only officer of the Thirty-Eighth, that took part in the charge, who

escaped unhurt. In September following, he was promoted to Captain in place of Captain Carpenter, deceased. After the capture of Fort Mahone, April 2d, 1865, he was accidentally wounded by one of the guns captured from the enemy. In July following, he was commissioned Lieutenant Colonel, but owing to the small number of men in the regiment, was unable to muster.

Captain Ballard was mustered out and returned to the State with the last detachment of the Thirty-Eighth.

FIRST LIEUTENANT JAMES M. SEARLES.

The subject of this sketch was born at Iowa City, in the State of Iowa, June 5th, 1864. In 1847, his parents removed to Grant county, Wisconsin. In 1852, the family removed to Madison, where it resided four years, and moved to Fox Lake, Dodge county. Here he resided four years, two of which he served as an apprentice to a marble cutter. During 1861 and 1862, he worked at his trade in Oshkosh, Winnebago county.

He enlisted, and was mustered into company C, of the 21st regiment of Wisconsin Volunteer Infantry, on the 5th of September, 1862, and six days after left the State with his regiment, to join the Army of the Ohio. On October 8th, he took part in the battle of Perryville, Ky. The 19th of that month he was detailed as Clerk in the office of the Medical Director of the Division. Although not taking part with his company, he was present at the battles of

Stone River, Hoover's Gap, Dug Gap, Chickamauga and Ringgold,

On the 9th of December, 1863, he was detailed as Clerk in the office of the Provost Marshal General of the Department of the Cumberland, and remained in that position until the 11th of March, 1864, when he received a furlough, and returned to Wisconsin. Shortly after his arrival in the State, he was commissioned Second Lieutenant of company A, of the Thirty-Eighth regiment, and mustered on the 15th of April.

On the 2d of May, he was detailed as Acting Quartermaster of the First Battalion, and accompanied it when it left next day for the front. On the arrival of the Second Battallion in Virginia, he was relieved from duty in the Quartermaster's Department, and reported back to his company. He remained with it from that time, except an absence of twenty days, and took an honorable part in all the movements and actions in which the regiment was subsequently engaged, and was honorobly discharged when the last detachment was mustered out.

———

LIEUT. G. W. PIER.

Lieut. G. W. Pier was born on the 1st day of July, 1844, at Fond du Lac, Wis., and was trained to the occupation of a farmer.

On the 31st of March, 1864, he enlisted, at Fond du Lac, as a private in company A, of the Thirty-Eighth Regiment. April 15th he was appointed

Corporal. He left the State with the First Battalion, and on the 28th of June was detailed for duty in the Q. M's office, where he remained until the 1st of September, when he was promoted to 2d Sergeant and returned to his company.

He participated in the battle of Poplar Spring Church, September 30th. Was promoted to Orderly Sergeant October 14th, and to Second Lieut. of his company, November 10th, 1864. He took part in all the subsequent movements of the Regiment. Was present, and bore an honorable part in the assault of the 2d of April, 1864, on Petersburg.

He was honorably discharged from service while the last detachment lay at Tennally Town in June 1865.

COMPANY B.

CAPT. FRANK A. HAYWARD.

Capt. Frank A. Hayward was born in Bridgeport, Wis., May 12th, 1844. He enlisted as a private in company G, of the 21st Regiment of Wis. Vol., and remained with it in all its movements and battles until November, 1863. He was thus engaged at the battles of Chaplain Hills, the affair at Jefferson's Pike, Hoover's Gap, and Chickamauga.

In January, 1863, he was promoted to Sergeant, and shortly after to the position of Orderly Sergernt of his company. In November, following, he was detailed on recruiting service in Wisconsin.

In March, 1864, having raised a sufficient number of men to entitle him to the position, he was commissioned First Lieutenant of company B, of the Thirty-

Eighth Regiment. When the first detachment left the State, he accompanied it, and took part in all its battles and marches. In the battle of the 17th of June, on the Norfolk railroad, he was wounded. His wound, however, was only sufficient to keep him from his company three days. He afterwards took part in the battles on the Weldon railroad and Poplar Spring Church.

On the promotion of Captain Roberts to Major, Lieut. Hayward was promoted to the Captaincy of his company. He subsequently took part in the battle of Hatcher's Run, October 27th, and the assault on Petersburg, April 2d, 1865, and in all subsequent movements of the Regiment.

Captain Hayward possessed unquestioned bravery, and was the strictest of strict disciplinarians. Fond of military life, because of the nicety and exactness of its rules, he made no allowances for the failures of those who, not only disliked it, but had no appreciation of its rules and distinctions, and often punished his men with inconsiderate severity for offenses against forms merely. As a consequence, he was enabled to bring his company to a high state of perfection in drill and in the manual of arms, but he failed to inspire the men with that confidence, respect and affection, the capacity to do which, after all, is the highest qualification of a commander.

In his private capacity, Captain Hayward is a social, genial companion, and honorable and high-minded in all his relations.

When Col. Bintliff and Major Roberts were mustered out, Captain Hayward was commissioned Ma-

M

jor, but for the same reasons given in the cases of Col. Pier and Capt. Ballard, was unable to muster.

——

✓ LIEUT. GEO. H. NICHOLS. *Des Moines Pat to 1?*

Lieut. Geo. H. Nichols, was born in Utica, in the State of New York, in 1838. The next year his parents removed to Wisconsin, and settled in the southern part of the State, residing for the last fifteen years in Kenosha. On the 5th of July, 1861, he enlisted as a private in the 1st regiment of Wisconsin cavalry, and took an active part in all the battles and marches in which that regiment participated while he belonged to it. On the 25th of October, 1862, he was commissioned Second Lieutenant in the 33d regiment Wis. Vol. Inft'y. While with this regiment he took part in the battles of Haines' Bluff and the siege of Vicksburg. After the capitulation of the latter place, he resigned and returned home.

Upon the subsequent call of the President for volunteers, he enlisted again as a private in company C, of the 16th Wis. Vols.

On the 8th of March, 1864, he was commissioned Second Lieutenant of company B, Thirty-Eighth Regiment, and accompanied the First Battalion when it went to the front. He was with the Regiment and took part in the battles on the Weldon railroad, Ream's Station and Poplar Spring Church. When Lieut. Hayward was promoted to Captain, Lieut. Nichols was advanced to the First Lieutenancy of his company.

He subsequently took part with the Regiment in its movements, and was present at the capture of Fort Mahone, April 2d, 1865, and behaved in a very creditable manner.

He remained with his company until the last detachment was mustered out, when he was honorably discharged.

LIEUT. SIMON C. STRICKLAND.

Lieut. Simon C. Strickland is a native of Chatauque county in the State of New York, and is about thirty-eight years of age. In 1840 the family moved to Barzetta, Trumbull county, Ohio. In September, 1863, Lieut. Strickland moved his family to Iola, Waupaca county, Wisconsin.

On the 18th of March, 1864, he enlisted in the Thirty-Eighth Regiment, and on the organization of company B, was appointed 5th Sergeant. He left the State with his company, and was present at the engagement of July 30th, and the battles on the Weldon railroad.

On the 15th of October, 1864, he was promoted to Second Lieutenant.

He subsequently remained with the Regiment, and was present at the storming of Fort Mahone. He remained with the last detachment until the 28th of of June, 1865, when he was mustered out and honorably discharged.

Lieutenant Strickland has red hair, blue eyes, and fair complexion, and is quiet and gentlemanly in his deportment.

COMPANY C.

CAPTAIN S. D. WOODWORTH.

We have not been able to obtain any data from which to write a sketch of the individual whose name heads this short article.

All that we have been able to learn of him is drawn from the records of the Regiment and personal observation during the few days we were in Camp Randall, and on the journey down to the front.

Captain Woodworth appeared to be about forty-three or forty-four years of age. He was about five feet ten or eleven inches in height, hair turning gray, blue eyes and fair complexion. In his intercourse with those under his command, he was rough, over-bearing and insolent. Report says that he was very little with his company; and during the summer obtained a leave of absence. When the Second Battalion went to the front, he accompanied it on his return from his leave of absence, and had charge of the recruits for the companies of the First Battalion. The climate, however, affected his health in such a manner that he found himself unable to proceed beyond City Point. On the 13th of October, he succeeded in obtaining a transfer to the Veteran Reserve Corps.

CAPT. L. B. WADDINGTON. *Dead*

Captain L. B. Waddington was born in Chatauque county, in the State of New York, and is now about thirty-one years of age. At the age of twenty-one, he came to Wisconsin, and settled in Argyle, Lafayette county, where he resided until he entered the military service.

He was commissioned First Lieutenant of company C, on the 14th of April, 1864, and accompanied the first detachment when it left the State. He was present in command of his company at the battles of the Mined Fort on the 30th of July, Weldon railroad, Poplar Spring Church, and at Hatcher's Run. He was promoted to Captain, November 14th, 1864. At the storming of Fort Mahone, he behaved with great credit to himself.

When the first detachment was mustered out, the most of the men transferred from that detachment were, of their own choice, assigned to his company. Captain Waddington came home with the last detachment, receiving an honorable discharge when it was mustered out.

LIEUT. WILLIAM N. WRIGHT.

Lieut. William N. Wright, was born in Louisville, St. Lawrance county, New York, on the first day of November, 1842.

In the fall of 1861, he removed to the State of Wisconsin. On the 27th of February, 1862, he enlist-

ed in company I, 27th Reg. Wis. Vol. Inf., and left the State with that regiment for the front, on the 31st of March, 1862, arriving in Tennessee in time to participate in the battle of Shiloh. He afterwards took part in the siege of Corinth. He was promoted to Corporal on the 14th of April. Was at the battle of Iuka, and also that of Corinth, at the latter of which he was wounded in the hand, and subsequently sent to the hospital at St. Louis, Mo., where he remained until the 22d of January, 1863, when he was discharged for disability.

On the 28th of December following, he re-enlisted in the same company and regiment and remained with it until about the 12th of March, 1864, when he received a commission promoting him to Second Lieutenant of company C, Thirty-Eighth Regiment Wis. Vol. Inf'y. Shortly after, he joined his company and went with it when the First Battalion left the State and went to the front. At Cold Harbor he was placed in command of the company. He was in the battle on the Norfork Railroad, Welden Railroad and Poplar Spring Church. On the 13th of November following, was promoted to First Lieutenant. He remained with the Regiment and was present at the storming of Fort Mahone, April 2d, 1865. At the time the last detachment was mustered out, he was honorably discharged from service. Lieut. Wright was a brave and efficient officer.

LIEUT. JOHN D. MILLION.

Lieut. John D. Million, was born in Wiota, Lafayette county, Wisconsin, on the 11th day of February, 1839. In 1856, he went to Kansas, as a Free State soldier, in Captain Whipple's company. He returned to Wisconsin, and enlisted in company C, Thirty-Eighth Regiment, Wisconsin Volunteer Infantry, on the 18th day of March, 1864. When the company was organized, he was appointed Second Sergeant. When the First Battalion left the State, he accompanied it, and took part in all its subsequent marches and battles. On the 11th of July, of the same year, he was promoted to First Sergeant, and on the 14th of November, following, to Second Lieutenant. On the 3d of July, 1865, he was honorably discharged from service. Lieut. Million is five feet seven inches in height, is strongly and compactly built, has black hair, black eyes and a dark complexion, and is a quiet and unpretending gentleman.

COMPANY D.

CAPT. JAMES WOODFORD.

We have no data from which to write a biographical sketch of this officer. His military career in the Thirty-Eighth Regiment, was of short duration. He is spoken of, by the men of his company, as possessing many fine and gentlemanly qualities. He

was commissioned Captain on the 8th of March, 1864, and accompanied the First Battalion when it went to the front. The feeble state of his health, however, soon compelled him to abandon the service, and on the 1st day of August, following, he resigned.

CAPTAIN WILLIAM H. FOSTER.

Captain Foster is a native of Winthrop, Maine. In the fall of 1844, he went to Mobile, Alabama, and in the spring of 1845, came to Wisconsin, and settled in Monroe, Green country. In 1853 he went to California and was absent three years. On the 22d of April, 1861, he enlisted to serve three years in the 3d regiment Wisconsin Volunteer Infantry. Took part in the battle of Bolivar, and was wounded in the right leg at the battle of Winchester, May 25th, 1862. He took part in Banks' retreat, Pope's campaign; was at the battle of Cedar Mountain, and was wounded in the hand at the battle of Antietam. He was subsequently in the battles of Chancellorville, Beverly Ford and at Gettysburgh.

In September, 1863, the Twelfth Corps, of which the Third Wisconsin formed a part, was transferred to the Western Department, and wintered in Tennessee. In the spring of 1864, under the command of General Sherman, it started in the grand campaign against Atlanta. At the battle near Dallas, Captain Foster was wounded in the left arm, in consequence of which he was sent to the hospital and afterwards transferred to Madison, Wisconsin,

where he was honorably discharged, his term of service having expired. On the 10th of September, 1864, he was commissioned First Lieutenant of company F, Thirty-Eighth Wisconsin Volunteer Infantry. On the 25th of December, following, was promoted Captain and transferred to company D, of that Regiment. On April 17th, 1865, was honorably discharged from the service by reason of disability. The record which Captain Foster has made for himself, is indeed a most honorable one.

CAPT. BENJAMIN S. KERR.

Captain Benjamin S. Kerr, is a native of Knox county, in the State of Ohio, and is about twenty-four years of age. His father was a farmer. When young Kerr was about four years old, his father removed to Wisconsin, and settled in Green county. At the age of thirteen he had the misfortune to lose his father, and was thus, in a great measure, thrown upon his own resources. He subsequently attended Platteville Academy, and was there at the time the war broke out. He continued in the Institution until the spring of 1862. Shortly after leaving it, he taught school for a few months, and in the spring of 1863, began the study of the Law, in the office of Judge Dunwiddie, of Monroe.

In the spring of 1864, he recruited a sufficient number of men to entitle him to a position as First Lieutenant, and was accordingly commissioned by Governor Lewis, on the 15th of April, in company

D. He left the State with the First Battalion, and participated in all the battles in which the Regiment has been engaged, except those on the Weldon railroad—he at that time being detailed on court martial at City Point. Lieutenant Kerr was in command of his company nearly all the time from June, 1865, until it was mustered out.

On the 8th of April, 1865, he was commissioned Captain, and mustered on the 13th of the same month. He remained with the last detachment, and was honorably discharged from service when it was mustered out.

Captain Kerr is a very quiet, unpretending gentleman, and as a soldier, attentive and assiduous in the discharge of his duties.

LIEUT. JAMES P. NICHOLS.

This officer is another of those whom we have been unable to obtain such data concerning, as would enable us to write an intelligent and reliable sketch. He is a about twenty-one or twenty-two years of age, and possessed of a rather slender constitution. He was commissioned Second Lieutenant of company D, on the 8th of March, 1864, and left for the front with the First Battalion. Soon after his arrival in Virginia, he was taken sick and went to hospital, where he remained all summer. Despairing of recovering his health in Virginia, he tendered his resignation on the 9th of June, which, however, was not accepted until sometime in October or November, following, when he was honorably discharged from the service.

LIEUT. CHAUNCEY W. HYATT.

Lieutenant Chauncey W. Hyatt was born in the county of Putnam, State of New York, on the 28th day of February, 1838. He removed to Wisconsin in May, 1855, and engaged in school-teaching. In March, 1859, he went to Missouri, where he remained until the fall of 1860, when he returned to Wisconsin.

In May, 1861, he enlisted in company C, 4th Wisconsin Volunteer Infantry, and was with that regiment in all its services. Was in the Eastern Shore campaign, under Lockwood; the New Orleans Expedition, under Butler; was twice up the river to Vicksburg, under Williams; assisted in digging the famous canal that was to make Vicksburg an inland city; was at the battle of Baton Rouge, after which he was sent to Chanty hospital, and about two months after discharged.

Upon being discharged, he returned to Wisconsin, where he remained until March 27th, 1864, when he re-enlisted, entering company D, of the Thirty-Eighth Regiment. He was appointed First Sergeant of the company, April 15th, and left the State with the First Battalion. He was with the Regiment, and participated in every engagement in which it took part, except those on the Weldon Railroad, at which time he was sick in hospital. He was promoted to Second Lieutenant, December 24th, 1864, and to First Lieutenant, May 13th, 1865.

Lieutenant Hyatt remained with the last detachment, and was honorably discharged when it was mustered out.

COMPANY E.

CAPTAIN NEWTON S. FERRIS.

Captain Newton S. Ferris was a native of the State of Ohio, and was, at the time he entered the military service, about thirty-eight years of age. His educational advantages, in early life, were such as could be obtained in the common schools of the community and the neighboring Academy. He subsequently engaged in teaching for a time; but, desiring to fit himself for the legal profession, he, just after his majority, if we are not mistaken, entered the law office of the Hon. William J. Bright, afterwards of New Lisbon, Wisconsin. His aptness and intelligence, as a student, was apparent in this as in all other studies, and his rapid progress was as gratifying to his preceptor and friends, as it was honorable to himself. Having finished his legal studies, in 1854 he came to Wisconsin, and opened a law office, in connection with Thomas Mason, at Quincy, in Adams county. For some time, while there, he held the office of County Judge. In 1859, he removed to New Lisbon, Juneau county, where he remained, in the practice of his profession, until the spring of 1864. In 1862, he was the democratic candidate, in the Sixth Congressional District, for Representative in Congress, but was defeated, the district giving the Union candidate a large majority.

In the spring of 1864, he was drafted, and though having the ability to commute, he refused to do it,

declaring that it had fallen to his lot to go into the military service, and that it was both his inclination and duty to do so.

In May following, he was commissioned First Lieutenant of company E, of the Thirty-Eighth Regiment, and soon after was promoted to Captain. In July he left the State with his company, to join the four companies already in the field before Petersburg, and reached them on the 26th of the same month. He gallantly led his company in the charge, at the battle of the Mined Fort four days afterwards, where he was killed.

Captain Ferris possessed talents of a high order. Without being an eloquent speaker, it may truly be said that few advocates could more closely enchain the attention of court or jury. He seemed to possess, in an eminent degree, the faculty of impressing upon those whom he addressed a sense of his own deep sincerity in all he said, and of imbuing them, for the time, with his own individuality.

In his private relations, he was honorable and straightforward; and in his family a kind and affectionate husband and father.

CAPT. FRANK G. HOLTON.

Captain Frank G. Holton, was born in the city of Milwaukee, Wisconsin, in 1846.

His boyhood was passed in attending schools, until 1861, when he entered the office of the Assistant Provost Marshal of the State, with the rank of Sergeant. When the office of the Assistant Provost

Marshal was vacated, he returned to his studies. Early in the summer of 1864, he was commissioned First Lieutenant of company E, Thirty-Eighth Regiment, and on the 20th of July left the State with his company, to join that part of the Regiment already in front of Petersburg, under command of Lieut. Col. Pier. On the 30th of the same month, he took part in the battle of the Mined Fort, and was severely wounded in the thigh, in consequence of which he was sent to the hospital, and afterwards received a leave of absence and returned home. On the last day of September, he started to return to the Regiment, but was taken sick on the way, and was unable to reach it until the last of October.

After that time, he remained with his command, but was scarcely ever able to perform full duty. When the first detachment was mustered out, he was honorably discharged and returned home. Captain Holton is a nephew of E. D. Holton, Esq., a prominent banker of Milwaukee.

FIRST LIEUT. FRANK M. PHELPS.

Lieut. Phelps, was born on the 23d day of December, 1844, at Three Rivers, in the State of Michigan. When he was three years of age, his father removed to Wisconsin, and settled in Milwaukee. In 1851, his father removed to Appleton. There he had the misfortune to lose his only remaining parent, his mother having died when he was one year old. From the death of his father, until 1861, he lived with an uncle. In September of that year, he en

listed in company C, Tenth Regiment of Wisconsin Volunteer Infantry, and left the State with that regiment, on the 9th of November, following, for Louisville, Kentucky. While in this regiment, he took part in the battles of Chaplin Hills, Stone River, Hoover's Gap, Chicamauga and Look-out Mountain, at the last of which he was seriously injured, by a log that rolled down the side of the mountain. Before fully recovering from this injury, he was commissioned, March 3d, 1864, as Second Lieutenant of company E, of the Thirty-Eighth Regiment, Wisconsin Volunteer Infantry, and left the State with that company, when it went to the front. He took part in the battle of the 30th of July, and those on the Weldon Railroad, in the last of which he was wounded in the hand. He afterwards took part in the battle of Popular Spring Church, and also the movement at Hatcher's Run. He was promoted to First Lieutenant, Sept. 6th, 1864, and was honorably discharged from service, when his company was mustered out.

LIEUT. ELI A. BENTLEY.

Lieut. Bentley, was born in Floyd, Oneida county, New York, November 18th, 1829. He removed to Wisconsin, in 1845. His business has, generally, been farming and lumbering. He entered the military service as a private, March 23d, 1864, in company E, of the Thirty-Eighth Regiment. He was promoted to Third Sergeant, on the 4th of the next June, and to First Sergeant, October 1st, and to

Second Lieutenant, on the 12th of the following November. He took part in all of the marches and battles in which his company was engaged, and was honorably discharged from service, at the time his company was mustered out. Lieut. Bentley was a good soldier and an efficient officer.

COMPANY F.

CAPT. ANDREW A. KELLY.

Captain Andrew A. Kelly, was born in the kingdom of Norway, on the 22d day of August, 1838, and received as good an education as the excellent Common Schools of that country afford.

In April, 1852, he emigrated from his native country and came to America, landing at Quebec on the 6th of June following. From that place he immediately proceeded to Chicago, where he remained for three months endeavoring to learn the English language, which he found a task of great difficulty. At the end of that time, finding his means exhausted, he went to Michigan, where he hired out to work in a mill for six dollars a month. "At first," says the Captain, "they put me to loading lumber on vessels, rolling logs, chopping and assisting to clear land. In fact, everything that was hard was my lot;" but as time passed, he soon gained the confidence of his employers, and as his knowledge of the customs and manner of business of our people increased, his wages were augmented and he was relieved from drudgery.

In May, 1856, he removed from Michigan to North-

western Wisconsin, settling on a farm in Alden, Polk county, where he continued to reside until after the war commenced.

In the summer of 1862, he enlisted as a private in the Thirtieth regiment, and served in the company commanded by Captain Sam Harriman, for twenty months, in enforcing the draft and picking up conscripts.

On the 16th of April, 1864, he was commissioned First Lieutenant of company F, in the Thirty-Eighth Regiment Wisconsin Volunteers, and was promoted to Captain on the 7th of September, following. When the last Battalion left the State, he accompaied it, and was with the Regiment in all its principal movements and battles until after the assault on Petersburg, April 2d, 1865, where he was severely, and at the time supposed mortally, wounded in the back and right side, during the storming of Fort Mahone.

Captain Kelly was remarkably temperate in his habits; abstaining entirely from all intoxicating drinks. It was, undoubtedly, owing to this trait of his character, that his life was saved at the time he was wounded. He is quiet and gentlemanly in his deportment, and an intelligent and faithful officer. His gallantry on the field was unsurpassed. Capt. Kelly was honorably discharged from service on the 6th of June, 1865, for disability, caused by the wounds received at Fort Mahone.

N

CAPT. E. W. PRIDE.

Captain E. W. Pride was born in the State of New York, in 1843, where a portion of his boyhood was passed. His parents subsequently removed to Wisconsin and settled in Brandon, Fond du Lac county, where young Pride was brought up on a farm.

In the spring of 1864, he earnestly set to work to raise men for the Thirty-Eighth Regiment, and on the 15th of April, was appointed Sergeant Major. When Lieutenant Foster was promoted to the rank of Captain, Sergeant Major Pride was commissioned First Lieutenant of company F, but that company having become reduced below the minimum number, he was unable to muster. At the assault on Fort Mahone, he behaved with coolness and bravery. A few days afterwards, he was reduced to the ranks for disobedience of orders of some kind, and returned to his company. When Captain Kelly was discharged, he was enabled to muster under his commission, and was shortly afterwards promoted to the rank of Captain. He was honorably discharged from service, July 25th, 1865.

LIEUT. JAMES W. PARKER.

Lieutenant James W. Parker was born in Cass county, in the State of Indiana, on the 1st day of June, 1840. Soon after his birth, his parents removed to Pittsburg, Pa., where they resided until he

was about twelve years of age, when they removed to Wisconsin, and settled in the town of Pleasant Springs, Dane county.

On the 29th of May, 1861, he enlisted in the Black Hawk Rifles. This company, however, owing to some misunderstanding, was disbanded shortly after, when he immediately re-enlisted in company B, 4th Wisconsin Volunteers. He accompanied that regiment in all its movements, and took part in all the battles of Grand Gulf, Bonnettecaire, Bisland, the numerous skirmishes in which his regiment was engaged, and the capture of New Orleans.

On the 8th of March, 1865, he was commissioned Second Lieutenant of company F, Thirty-Eighth Regiment. He joined his new command and was mustered into service on the 26th of April.

He left the State with the last Battalion and was present with the Regiment in all its subsequent movements. On the 2d of April, during the assault on Petersburg, he had charge of the picket line and made a charge across upon the enemy's pickets and captured several prisoners. When Lieutenant Pride was promoted to Captain, Lieutenant Parker was advanced to the rank of First Lieutenant.

He remained with the last detachment, and was honorably discharged from service when it was mustered out.

COMPANY G.

CAPT. R. F. BECKWITH. *Dead!*

Captain Reuben F. Beckwith is a native of the State of Maine, from which he removed to the State of Wisconsin, and settled in Oconto county, where he engaged in lumbering.

Upon the breaking out of the war he enlisted in a company of Wisconsin cavalry, and was for some time in active service in the Southwest.

In September, 1864, he was commissioned Captain of company G, Thirty-Eighth Regiment. When the Second Battalion left the State, he accompanied it, and subsequently took part in all the movements and battles in which the Regiment was engaged.

During the months of February and March, 1865, he was entrusted with the repairing and fitting up of the picket line in front of the Regiment, and performed that important duty in a very satisfactory manner.

Captain Beckwith was not far from forty years of age when he joined the Thirty-Eighth Regiment. He is about five feet nine inches in height, has light brown hair, grayish blue eyes, a very fair complexion, and is possessd of great decision and force of character. In his temper he is imperious and self willed, but brave and fond of excitement and adventure.

LIEUT. WILLIAM E. MAXSON.

The subject of this sketch was born in Friendship Allegany county, New York, in the year 1837. When he was twelve years of age his father removed to Wisconsin and settled in the south-eastern part of Dane county.

At the age of nineteen, with the consent of his father, he left home for the purpose of making his own fortune in the world. He possesses a naturally inventive mind, and was, in connection with an older brother, the first to invent and patent a successful sack-fastener.

In 1856, he entered Alford University, New York, where he pursued his studies between two and three years, after which, in connection with his brother, he commenced the publication in that place of "The New Era," a literary paper. The enterprise flourished for nearly a year, when, upon hearing of the " Fall of Fort Sumter," he and his brother, with thirteen college students, bade good-bye to friends and home and started for Washington. He enlisted in the 23d, New York Volunteers Infantry, then rapidly organizing, and with that regiment, took part in the battles of Rappahannock Station, White Sulphur Springs, Gainesville, Bull Run, Chantilla, South Mountain, Antietam and Fredricksburg. The two years for which he had enlisted having expired, he was discharged in May, 1863. During the hours off duty he compiled a history of the two years campaign of his regiment, entitled "Camp

Fires of the Twenty-Third," which he published in May, 1863.

In the following autumn he went to Kansas City, Missouri and afterwards to Wisconsin.

During the summer of 1864, he raised a company of men, for the 42d Wisconsin Volunteers, but failing to get into that Regiment, entered the Thirty-Eighth Regiment, with sixty-six of his men, and was commissioned First Lieutenant of company G.

When the Second Battalion left the State, he accompanied it, and was with the Regiment in all of its movements, until December following, when he was detailed on the staff of Col. Sam. Harriman, commanding the First Brigade, First Division, Ninth A. C., as Pioneer Officer, in which capacity he took part in the assault on Fort Mahone, April 2d, 1865. He remained upon the staff of Col. Harriman, until about the first of June, following, when he was relieved, and returned to his company.

When his company was mustered out he was honorably discharged from service. Lieut. Maxson was a conscientious and intelligent officer, and gave all the powers of his mind to the faithful discharge of his duties.

———

LIEUT. CHARLES S. WOOD.

Lieut. Wood was born in the State of New York, in the year 1845. The period at which he removed to the State of Wisconsin is unknown to us; but upon the first call for troops we find him, in June 1861, although only sixteen years of age, entering

the service as a private in the 5th Wisconsin Volunteers, in which organization he served two years and ten months.

During that time he took part with his regiment in the battles of Williamsburg, Yorktown, Golden's Farm—where he was slightly wounded in the left leg—Second battle of Bull's Run, First and Second battles of Fredericksburg—at the latter of which he was wounded with three balls in the left hip—Chancellorville—where he was slightly wounded in the left arm—Antietam, Gettysburg and Cedar Mountain.

In April, 1864, he was commissioned Second Lieutenant of Company G, Thirty-Eighth Regiment Wisconsin Volunteers. When the second Battallion left the State, he accompanied it, and remained with the Regiment during all its subsequent movements and battles until the second of April, 1865. At the storming of Fort Mahone on that day, he was severely wounded in the left hand and thigh, while gallantly leading his company.

His conduct was so conspicuous on this occasion, that on the second of June following, he was for that cause breveted First Lieutenant.

Lieutenant Wood was honorably discharged from service, at the time the First detachment was mustered out.

COMPANY II.
CAPT. D. W. COREY.

This officer is a resident of Monroe, Green county, Wisconsin, and at the time he entered the Thirty-Eighth Regiment, we should judge, about thirty-five or thirty-six years of age. In the summer of 1864, he raised a company for the Thirty-Eighth, and in September was commissioned its Captain, his company being designated as II.

When the Second Battalion left the State, he accompanied it to the front. In November, following, he was taken sick and went to the hospital, from which he never returned to duty. Sometime during the latter part of the next winter, he tendered his resignation, and was discharged for disability.

—

CAPT. B. F. FREES.

Captain Frees was born in Orono, Penobscot county, Maine, on the 3d day of August, 1846.

His father was a merchant. In the fall of 1856, his parents moved to Monroe, Wisconsin, where he resided until August, 1863, when he removed to Whitewater, Jefferson county.

He enlisted in the Thirty-Eighth Regiment Wisconsin Volunteers as a private, on the 27th of August, 1864, and was commissioned First Lieutenant of company II, on the 6th of September, following.

When the Second Battalion left the State, he went

with it to the front, and remained with his company during all the subsequent operations and movements of the Regiment.

On the 14th of January, 1865, he was promoted to Captain in place of Captain Corey who had been discharged for disability.

At the assault on Petersburg he behaved with great gallantry. Captain Frees was a brave and accomplished officer, and was very popular with his brother officers and the men of his command.

———

LIEUT. JAMES B. HETH, Jr.

Lieutenant Heth was born on the 19th day of February, 1841, in the city of Buffalo, N. Y.

In 1855, his father removed his family to Milwaukee, Wisconsin, where the subject of this sketch continues to reside.

On the 11th of August, 1862, he enlisted in company B, 24th Wisconsin Volunteers, and with that regiment left the State for the seat of war, on the 5th of the next month.

He participated in all the marches and movements of that regiment, and was with it in the battles of Chaplin Hills, Stone River, Chickamauga and Mission Ridge.

On the 8th of March, 1864, he was promoted to Second Lieutenant of company H, Thirty-Eighth Regiment Wisconsin Volunteers.

He accompanied the Second Battalion when it left the State for the front, and was with the Regiment in all of its subsequent movements, and took part

with it in the battle of Hatcher's Run. On the 14th of January, 1865, he was promoted to First Lieutenant of his company.

He took part in the assault on Fort Mahone, April 2d, 1865, where he behaved with great coolness and gallantry.

LIEUT. WILLIAM ADAMS.

Lieutenant Adams was born on the 5th of January, 1835, in Bedford county, Penn.

Subsequently his parents moved to Hardin county, Ohio, and afterwards to Cohocton county in the same State, where he resided till the fall of 1854, when he removed to the State of Wisconsin and settled in Green county. In the spring of 1863, he went to California, from which he returned in the fall of the same year.

On the 5th of August, 1864, he enlisted in the Thirty-Eighth Regiment Wisconsin Volunteers, and when company H was organized was promoted to Orderly Sergeant.

He left the State with his company when it went to Virginia and took part in all of the subsequent movements and battles of the Regiment. He was at the battle of Hatcher's Run. On the 14th of January, 1865 he was promoted to Second Lieutenant of his company. He took part in the assault on Fort Mahone, April 2nd, 1865. Lieut. Adams is five feet ten inches in height, has fair complexion, blue eyes, auburn hair and is about thirty years of age. His present home is Monroe, Green county, Wisconsin.

COMPANY I.

CAPTAIN HENRY H. COLMAN.

Captain Colman was born in Yates county, New York, on the 20th day of August, 1825. He removed to the State of Ohio in 1832 and remained there until the winter 1834, when he removed to Washtenaw county, Michagan, where he resided until 1844. That year he removed to Wisconsin and settled in Rock county, where he has resided ever since, except a part of 1852 and 1853 spent in California.

On his return from that State, he established himself in the mercantile business, which he followed until 1860, when he went to Colorada Territory and was absent about two years. On his return he entered the dry goods house of A. O. K. Bennett.

On the 1st of August, 1864, he enlisted as a private in the Thirty-Eighth Regiment, and immediately commenced to raise a company.

On the 21st of September, he was commissioned Captain of Company I, of that Regiment, and left the next day with his company for Virginia. Shortly after the arrival of the Battalion in Virginia, the climate, exposure and fatigue which he, in common with all the rest of the command, was compelled to undergo, so affected his health that he found himself compelled to go to the hospital, where he remained until some time in the month of February, 1865, when having recovered, he returned to his command.

At the storming of Fort Mahone, April 2nd, 1865,

he took part and showed himself possessed of a coolness and courage hardly surpassed.

Capt. Colman was honorably discharged from the service when the first detachment was mustered out.

LIEUT. JOEL N. STRAIGHT.

Lieutenant Straight was born on the 16th of June, 1832, in the town of Williamson, Wayne county, N. Y.

He came to the State of Wisconsin at the age of fifteen and settled in Neosho, Dodge county, where he was joined the next year by his parents.

In 1851, he went to Milwaukee and apprenticed himself to learn the jeweller and watchmaker's trade.

He entered the military service as a private on the 1st day of August, 1861, in company H, 12th regiment Wisconsin Volunteers. In October following, he was transferred to the regimental band, and in that capacity was with it in all of its marches and movements from the time it left the State until April 14th, 1864.

During that time the Regiment was engaged in the battles of Tallahatchie, Hernando, Grand Gulf, Fort Gibson, Raymond, Champion Hills and Vicksburgh, at the latter of which he was slightly wounded in the neck.

On the 14th of April, 1864, he was discharged for disability.

He was commissioned First Lieutenant of company I, Thirty-Eighth Regiment Wisconsin Volun-

teers on the 15th day of September, following, and accompanied the Second Battalion when it went to the front.

He remained with his regiment during all its subsequent movements and actions till his company was mustered out, when he was honorably discharged from the service.

LIEUT. CHARLES O. HOYT.

Lieutenant Hoyt was born at Framingham, Middlesex county, Mass., on the 27th day of September, 1839.

His father was a Physician and Surgeon, and served in that capacity during the Mexican War, with the 1st Massachusetts Volunteers, and during the late Rebellion, with the 30th Wisconsin Volunteers.

In 1846, the family removed to Charlestown, Mass., and two years later, to St. Croix Falls, Wisconsin.

Young Hoyt was partly educated at Platteville Academy, Grant county, and partly at St. Paul College, Minn.

He entered the army the 19th of April, 1861, as a private in company G, 4th Wisconsin Volunteers, in which company he served until promoted to Second Lieutenant of company I, Thirty-Eighth Regiment.

During the time that he was in the 4th regiment, he took part in the first siege of Vicksburg, battles of Baton Rouge, Clinton, and the siege of Fort Hudson.

He was promoted to Second Lieutenant of company

I, Thirty-Eighth Regiment Wisconsin Volunteers, on the 8th of March, 1864. He left the State with the Second Battalion, and participated in all of the subsequent movements of the Regiment.

He participated in the battle of Hatcher's Run, and in the storming of Fort Mahone, April 2d, 1865.

He behaved with coolness and courage, and was honorably discharged from service when his company was mustered out.

COMPANY K.

CAPT. THOMAS B. MARSDEN.

Captain Thomas B. Marsden was born in Yorkshire, England, October 22d, 1824. His parents immigrated to the United States in June, 1824, and settled in Wayne county, N. Y. In August, following, his father died. A few years after his father's death, his mother again married, and in 1831, her husband and herself, taking her son with them, removed to Michigan. The family, in 1836, came to Wisconsin, and settled in the town of Menomonee, Waukesha county. There he made it his home, until he was eighteen years old, when he began an apprenticeship to the trade of manufacturing fanning-mills. Having finished his apprenticeship, he established himself in the business of manufacturing such mills. In 1849, he was married to Miss Minerva Nye, of Menomonee, and two years later removed to Appleton, where he continued the manufacture of mills. In 1855, he removed to Preston, Adams

county, where he remained about eighteen months, and then settled in Friendship in the same county, where he continues to reside.

In 1857, he was elected chairman of the Board of Supervisors of his town, and member of the County Board of Supervisors. In 1858, he was elected Clerk of the County Board of Supervisors, and was subsequently honored with two successive re-elections to the same office.

On the 31st of July, 1864, having determined to enter the army, he enlisted, as private in the Thirty-Eighth Regiment. Having a recruiting commission, he immediately, in connection with S. W. Pierce, began the work of raising a company of men in Adams county. In this he was successful, and on the 8th of September, following, was commissioned Captain of company K, of the Thirty-Eighth Regiment. He accompanied the Second Battalion, when it left the State, for the theater of active operations, and took an active part in all the subsequent movements of the Regiment. He took part in the battle of Hatcher's Run, and the assault on Fort Mahone, where he behaved with coolness and intrepidity. When the first detachment was mustered out, it returned to the State, under his command. He was honorably discharged, at the same time. At the General Election, 1865, he was elected to represent the Assembly district, in which he resides, in the next State Legislature.

Capt. Marsden, is a gentleman of fine and commanding personal appearance, and was universally popular in the Regiment.

LIEUT. S. W. PIERCE.

Lieut. Pierce was born in Cattaraugus county, N. Y., on the 7th of March, 1831. When he was about a year old, however, his parents removed to Monroe county, in the same State. There his parents resided and his boyhood was passed until his thirteenth year, when he met with the irreparable loss of his father, who died after a long illness, leaving the family in very destitute circumstances. He never forgot, however, the noble example of an honorable life that his father left him — a legacy far more precious than gold. He never had a prouder moment than when, a few years since, he heard a gentleman who had known his father intimately for years, in all the relations of life say, "your father was the most honorable man I ever knew; I do not believe he was ever guilty of a dishonorable action." It is that example that, through all the years of his boyhood, acted as talisman to save him from the temptations and vices that throng around the paths of an unprotected youth.

The next summer he lived with an uncle of his mother's, where his only compensation for months of hard labor was what food he wanted to eat. That fall he secured a situation in Rochester, N. Y., where, by working out of school hours, he could pay for his board and clothes. Here he remained nearly a year attending school. From that time until he was nineteen years old, his time was spent alternately working on a farm and attending school. Having a pas-

sion for the study of the law he, during this time, read every work on that subject he was able to procure.

In 1855, he came to Wisconsin and settled in Cascade, Adams county, and two years later formed a law-partnership with H. P. Brown, Esq. The connection, however, was dissolved by mutual consent, after a few months, as he desired to remove to Friendship and open a law office there, which he did in December, 1857, and has resided there ever since.

In 1861, he was elected County Judge, without opposition, and held the office until entering the army, when he resigned.

In April, 1861, he began the publication of the Adams County *Press*, a weekly newspaper, which is now in a flourishing and prosperous condition.

July 31st, 1864, enlisted as a private in the Thirty-Eighth Regiment, and in connection with Capt. Marsden, raised Company K, of that Regiment, and was commissioned First Lieutenant of the company, on the 12th of September. He was never absent from his company a day, from the time it reached the front until it was mustered out.

Was honorably discharged from service on the 2d day of June, 1865.

———

LIEUT. FRED. T. ZETTELER.

Lieut. Fred. T. Zetteler, was born in Flushing, in the kingdom of the Netherlands, on the 8th day of December, 1843. In 1847, his parents removed to the United States, and settled in Milwaukee Wis-

o

In 1854, his parents moved to Madison, where they resided six or seven years, and then returned to Milwaukee. In 1860, he apprenticed himself to learn the Tinsmith's trade. August 12th, 1864, he enlisted in Capt. Von Bombach's company, (C), of the 24th Regiment, Wisconsin Volunteers. He served with that Regiment, until he was promoted. He took part in the battles of Chaplin Hills and Stone River, at the latter of which he was wounded and taken prisoner. He was treated very kindly by the rebels, except that he, nor any of his comrades were furnished enough to eat, one small biscuit being the ration allowed each day. On the succeeding Sunday, after his capture, he was retaken by our forces, and sent to the hospital at Nashville, and from there was successively sent to the hospital at West End, and to Cincinnati. His wound having nearly healed, on the 15th of March he requested to be sent to his Regiment, to which he reported for duty, on the 4th of April. The Regiment was then at Murfreesboro. He subsequently took part in the battles of Chickamauga and Mission Ridge, and all the marches and skirmishes in which his Regiment was engaged, until the 1st of April, 1864, when he received a commission, dated March 8th, promoting him to Second Lieutenant of company K, Thirty-Eighth Regiment, for gallant and meritorious conduct. He was mustered April 13th, and ordered to Milwaukee on recruiting service. He joined the Regiment in September, with the Second Battalion, and remained with it, and took part in all its subsequent movements and battles, and was honorably discharged from service when his company was mustered out.

RECORD

OF

ENLISTED MEN.

.

COMPANY A.—MUSTERED OUT JULY 25TH, 1865.

NAMES.	AGE.	WHERE BORN.	RESIDENCE.	OCCUPATION.	REMARKS.
SERGEANTS.					
1st E. H. Little	19	New York	Fond du Lac	Clerk	Slightly wounded, June 17, '64. Reduced Aug. 9, '64. Discharged January 5, 1865.
2d Isaac Burch	31	Kentucky	"	Engraver	
3d Geo W Bedbury	24	New York	"	Engineer	Severely wounded June 20, '64. Discharged Dec. 23, 1864.
4th Henry A Chase	20	Vermont	Fond du Lac	Medical Student	
5th J M Wells	36	Ohio	Fond du Lac	Cooper	
CORPORALS.					
W J Stewart	43	Ireland	Fond du Lac	Merchant	Slightly wounded June 18, '64.
H M Soper	22	Wisconsin	"	Merchant	Severely wounded June 17, '64.
W H Weber	27	Germany	"	Tailor	Died in Chester Hospital, June 22, 1864.
A A Dye	18	Wisconsin	Byron, F du Lac Co	Student	Slightly wounded, June 18, '64.
John Irving	44	Scotland	Fond du Lac	Shoemaker	Wounded July 1864. Dis. Dec. 30, 1864.
J V Jewell	44	New York	Fond du Lac	Miner	
Geo M Pier	19	Wisconsin	Byron, F du Lac Co	Merchant	
W W Wilcox	27	New York	Fond du Lac	Farmer	Wounded left leg, June 17, '64.
MUSICIANS.					
Charles E Sears	18	Wisconsin	Byron, F du Lac Co	Farmer	Died in Washington, Sept. 25, '64.
Ela C Waters	14	New York	Fond du Lac	Student	

COMPANY A.—[CONTINUED.]

PRIVATES.

NAMES.	AGE.	WHERE BORN.	RESIDENCE.	OCCUPATION.	REMARKS.
Adams, Hackley	17	Wisconsin	Byron	Student	Killed at Cold Harbor, Va., June, 12, 1864.
Ames, John	33	"	Fond du Lac	Farmer	Discharged for disability April 29th, 1865.
Arnold, John	41	Germany	Schleswig, Wis	"	Mortally wounded June 17th, 1864. Died June 29, 1864.
Albert, Charles	21		Lomira, Dodge Co	"	Mortally wounded June 17, '64. [Died June 26, 1864.
Braford, W H	18	Wisconsin	Fond du Lac	"	
Burrows, D V	23	Michigan	Byron,F du LacCo	"	
Besaw, Martin	17	New York	Fond du Lac	"	
Baker, Ernst	18	Germany	Schleswig	Shoemaker	Severely wounded July 19, '64. Right leg amputated.
Brandt, Wm	43	Prussia	Madison	Farmer	Died in 3d Div. 9th A. C. Hospital, August 31, 1864.
Beardsley, J H	20	Vermont	Manston, Wis	"	Discharged for disability.
Bennett, A F	18	New York	Madison	"	Missing in action July 30, 1864.
Bramers, Henry	23	"	Milwaukee, Wis	Book-keeper	Deserted May 3d, '64,at Madison.
Childs, Chas F	18	New Jersey	Fond du Lac	Student	Killed June 19, '64, on Norfolk Railroad.
Currier, Geo W	24	New York	Rosendale, Wis	Farmer	Killed July 30, 1864, at Mined Ft
Cummings, N	44	Canada	Fond du Lac	"	Taken prisoner July 30, 1864.
Divers, J C	32	New Jersey	Byron,F du LacCo	Teacher	Wounded June 17. Died 18, '64.
Dana, Chas O	18	New York	Manston, Wis	Laborer	

Name	Age	Birthplace	Residence	Occupation	Remarks
Ellenbecker, N	22	Germany	Belgium, Wis	Carpenter	Severely wounded, June 28th. Transferred to Invalid Corps.
Enos, S C	44	New York	Milwaukee, Wis	Farmer	
Ford, Jno C	34	Ireland	Fond du Lac	Teacher	Transferred to Co. F, August 26th, 1864.
Foley, John	18	Canada	Neenah	Farmer	Died in hospital at Madison, [June, 1864.
Franke, August	23	Germany	Hustisford, Wis	"	
Greene, J C	27	New York	Manitowoc, Wis	"	Slightly wou'd in knee April 2d.
Groetzinger, Conrad	36	Germany	Schleswig	"	Promoted Corporal Jan. 1, '65.
Hudson, H A	19	New York	Byron, F'd u Lac Co	Farmer	Deserted at Madison, May 3, '64.
Hurley, Wm	22	Ohio	Milwaukee, Wis	"	
Holl, Lyman	29	New York	Auburn, Wis	"	
Hatch, Alanson	30	Vermont	Milwaukee, Wis	"	
Hays, J H	23	Indiana	"	"	
Harvey, H E	17	New York	Wisconsin	Student	Died June 12, '64, in Columbia [Hospital, Washington.
Hutchinson, J W	17	Ohio	Fond du Lac	Farmer	Wounded, June 20, 1864.
Holl, Robert	21	"	Chilton, Wis	"	Wounded, Sept. 30, battle of [Poplar Spring Church. Discharged May 20, 1864.
Harrison, Ole	37	Norway	Palmyra, Wis	"	Died Nov. 3, 1864, in Harwood, [Hospital, Washington, D. C.
Heffren, Chris.	20	Ireland	"	Boiler-maker	Promoted to Hospital Steward, [vice Prudent.
Hilliard, James	44	"	Marquette	Farmer	
Jewett, J J	29	N.Hampshire	Milwaukee	Druggist	
Kane, John	18	New York	Neenah	Laborer	
Kelk, Henry	16	"	Sheboygan		
King, Martin	33	Ireland	Madison	Farmer	Promoted Corporal Jan. 1st, '65.
Lake, W W	38	New York	Oshkosh	"	Trans'd to V. R. C. Feb 2, '65.
Lahore, Edwin	26	Vermont	Columbus	Laborer	Dis. for disability, March 20, '65.
Lester, Joseph	21	Pennsylvania	Pennsylvania	Farmer	

COMPANY A.—[CONTINUED.]

NAMES.	AGE.	WHERE BORN.	RESIDENCE.	OCCUPATION.	REMARKS.
Lockhart, J N	25	Indiana	Fond du Lac Co	Teacher	Q. M. S. April 15, 1864.
Nelson, Edward	18	Wisconsin	Palmyra, Wis	Farmer	Wounded June 17, 1864.
O'Malley Michael	36	Ireland	Madison	Laborer	Wounded June 17, '64, slightly in hand.
Odell, L G	24	New York	Delavan, Wis	Cooper	Promoted to Corp'l Sept. 1, '64.
Olger, Geo W	18	"	Kingston, Wis	Farmer	
Prudent, H R	31	Prussia	Fond du Lac	Druggist	Promoted to hospital steward April 15, 1864. Reduced and deserted Dec. 9, 1864.
Pride, E W	21	New York	Brandon, Wis	Farmer	S. M., April 15th 1864.
Pixley, Henry	23	Indiana	"	"	Deserted at Madison, May 3. '64.
Peckham, W H	17	New York	Milwaukee	Student	Promoted 2nd Lieut., in 44th Wis. Vols. Feb. 20, 1865.
Power, Michael	44	Ireland	Marquette, Wis	Farmer	Wounded July 3, 1864, near [Petersburg.
Robbins, C W	17	New York	Byron, F du Lac Co	"	
Ramsey, Geo W	26	"	Berlin	"	Discharged in August, 1864, [before leaving the State.
Ribble, D P	16	Wisconsin	Fond du Lac	Student	
Rundel, G A	16	New York	"	"	
Ruppert, M	18	Germany	Belgium	Farmer	
Rayner, D B	42	New York	Saukville, Wis	"	Promoted Corporal Jun 1st, '65
Remington, J W	18	Wisconsin	Mauston, Wis	"	
Schaefer, Conrad	40	Germany	Schleswig	Farmer	Died in 3d Div 9th A C hospital, August 18, 1864.
Schubert, A H	18	"	"	Blacksmith	Wounded June 17, 1864, and Sept. 30, severely.
Thilke, F J	18	"	Lomira, Dodge Co	Farmer	

Name	Age	Birthplace	Residence	Occupation	Remarks
Taylor, E M	16	Wisconsin	Byron, F du Lac Co	"	
Taylor, B	40	New York	"	"	
Taylor, Chas F	26	"	Saukville, Wis	Blacksmith	Discharged Dec. 24, 1864.
Fred, Z	42	"	Columbus, Wis	Clerk	Died at City Point Va., October 8, 1864.
Wright, J T	42	"	Oakfield	Shoemaker	
Woodard, J A	33	Vermont	Fond du Lac	Farmer	
Williams, W S	20	Wales	Waupaca, Wis	Book-keeper	

RECRUITS.

Name	Age	Birthplace	Residence	Occupation	Remarks
Andrus, Jno P	20	Mass	Auburn, Wis	Farmer	
Ayres, Geo	39	Germany	Fond du Lac	Carpenter	
Conklin, Daniel	23	Wisconsin	"	Farmer	
Gray, Jno	35	Ireland	Eden. F du Lac Co	"	
Hammond, Samuel	30	Maine	Oshkosh	"	Wounded slightly in wrist April [2d], 1865.
Hammond W B	18	"	"	"	
Launen, Michael	44	Mass	Berlin	Carpenter	
Long, Elias	43	New York	Madison, Wis	Farmer	
McCormick, Jas	30	Ireland	Lynxville "	"	
Ostrum, Jno C.	34	New York	Aurora	"	Hit with spent musket ball, on [left lung, April 2nd, 1865.
Pixley, Willis C.	39	Connecticut	Oshkosh	Laborer	
Sackett, F H	17	Ohio	Eden, Wis	Farmer	
Stowell, Ed L	18	Illinois	Madison, Wis	Clerk	
Titus, Jos	32	New York	Fond du Lac	Farmer	
Thomas, Lorenzo	44	"	Racine	Mason	
Tallmadge, H F	18	Wisconsin	Fond du Lac	Farmer	Promoted Color Corp May 1, '65.
Vanguilder, A	40	New York	"	"	
Whitney E J	37	"	Eden, Wis	Wagon-maker	
Wiley, J H	32	Pennsylvania	Berlin	Painter	

COMPANY B.—MUSTERED OUT JULY 25TH, 1865.

NAMES.	AGE.	WHERE BORN.	RESIDENCE.	OCCUPATION.	REMARKS.
SERGEANTS.					
1st Joseph S Burnham	33	Vermont	Iola, Wis	Farmer	Killed in action July 30, 1864.
2d George Hinton	32	Ohio	New Lisbon, Wis	"	Wounded in right arm April 2nd, [1865. Arm amputated. Discharged May 2, 1865.
3d William C Pitcher	38	New York	Waupaca	Shoemaker	Promoted 2nd Sergt. Oct. 7, '64.
4th Abraham Rode	28	Penn	Rushford, Wis	Farmer	Promoted 1st Sergt. June 1, '65.
5th S C Strickland	33	New York	Iola, Wis	Carpenter	Promoted 1st Sergt. Sept. 1st, [1864. Promoted 2nd. Lieut. [Oct. 7, 1864.
CORPORALS.					
Isaac Simcock	28	England	Waupaca, Wis	Tinsmith	Taken prisoner July 30, 1864.
Robert Blair	34	Ireland	Lenark, Wis	Farmer	
Thomas Parks	43	Penn	New Lisbon, Wis	"	Promoted Sergt. May 25, 1865.
Henry Blair	28	Ireland	Lenark, Wis	"	Promoted Sergt. Oct. 1, 1864
Samuel Norton	45	New York	Little Wolf, Wis	"	
Henry Chandler	23	N Hampshire	Iola, Wis	Miner	Died in hospital, August 1864.
Julius M Dutton	17	New York	Waupaca, Wis	Carpenter	Wounded in action, July 30, 1864. Dis. June 21, 1865.
Franklin McReynolds	18	Wisconsin	Fennimore	Farmer	
PRIVATES.					
Alderman, W R	20	Indiana	Little River, Wis	Farmer	Wounded June 17, 1864.
Alderman, James	18	do	"	"	Died at Post hospital, Madison, May 18, 1864.

Name	Age	Birthplace	Residence	Occupation	Remarks
Adams Augustus	23	Canada	Peshtigo, Wis	Laborer	Killed in action June 26, 1864.
Buck, Amos P	36	Ohio	Farmington	Carpenter	Wounded in foot, Aug. 13, '64. Discharged May 10, 1865.
Brand, James S	21	New York	Iola, Wis	Farmer	Discharged May 19, 1865.
Bailey, Frank	24	Wisconsin	Peshtigo, Wis	Lumberman	Died Auger hospital Aug. 13, '65.
Borner, Fred	33	Prussia	do Wis	do	Promoted to Corp. Dec.1st, 1864.
Conway, John	26	Ireland	do Wis	Farmer	Taken prisoner, July 30, 1864. Died in rebel prison, at Danville, Va., Dec. 29, 1864.
Colburn, J G	16	Vermont	Waupaca, Wis	do	Died in hospital, June 29, '64.
Cannady, J	40	New York	Little Wolf, Wis	do	
Cain, W A	20	Maine	St. Lawrence Wis	do	
Dickey, J W	32	N Hampshire	New Lisbon, Wis	do	Killed in action, June 17, 1864.
Dempsey, S H	24	Penn	Fennimore, Wis	do	
Eastman, A D	18	Illinois	Little River, Wis	do	
Emerson, J	17	New York	Lind, Waupaca Co	do	
Fisher, E	18	do	Waupaca	Musician	Wounded in action, June 24 '61.
Foss, Daniel	16	Maine	Royalton	Lumberman	
Flint, M D	23	Vermont	Iola	Book-keeper	Promoted to Com. Serg't, April 1st, 1865.
Gerard, S W	23	Ohio	Waupaca	Carpenter	Wounded in action June 17, '64. Discharged Dec 2, 1864.
Gregory, J S	30	New York	do	Farmer	Killed in action July 30, 1864.
Griswold, George	19	Illinois	Fennimore	do	Wounded in action Aug. 19, '64.
Griswold, Gaylord	18	Wisconsin	do	do	Wounded June 17, 1864.
Harvey, M.	41	England	Farmington, Wis	do	Promoted Corporal Nov. 1, '64. Discharged May 20, 1865.
Hinton, Thos J	22	Illinois	Orange, Juneau Co	do	Killed in action, July 30, 1864.
Hunter, Mat	19	Penn	Fennimore, Wis	do	

COMPANY B.—[CONTINUED.]

NAMES.	AGE.	WHERE BORN.	RESIDENCE.	OCCUPATION.	REMARKS.
Hinchliff, J	24	England	Omro, Wis	Farmer	Promoted to Corporal July 1, '65
Jones, J D	29	New York	Iola, Wis	Miner	Appointed Corporal Sept. 1, '64.
Loomis, J N	44	"	Kaukauna, Wis	Farmer	Promoted to Serg't, June 1, '65
Leopold, A	26	Bavaria	Ellington, Wis	do	Deserted May 8, 1864.
Leach, Alex	21	Ireland		do	Wounded in action, July 30, '64.
Murray, Wm	34	"	Weyauwega, Wis	do	Discharged Jan. 20, 1865.
Morse, S S	36	Vermont	Waupaca, Wis	do	Died in September, 1864.
Mitchell, O W	37	New York	Amherst, Wis	Lumberman	Taken prisoner July 30, 1864. [Died in rebel prison, at Dan-[ville, Va., Nov. 25th, 1864.
McOwen, W	20	New York	Waupaca, Wis	Farmer	Wounded in action July 30, '64.
Mason, D L	15	Vermont	Beaver Dam	do	[Leg amput'ed. Dis.June11,'65.
Norton, G W	20	New York	Little Wolf, do	do	Wounded on picket, Dec. 15, 1861. Dis. May 24, 1865.
Osborne, Ed J	21	do	Lenark Wis	do	Died while home on furlough, [about Nov. 10, 1861.
Pierce, C W	46	do	to	do	Wounded in action July 30, '64.
Phew, Wm	72	Ohio	Farmington, Wis	do	Missing in action July 17, 1864.
Perkins, J B	19	New York	Waupaca, do	Wheel-wright	
Parks, S E B	33	Penn	Fountain, do	Farmer	
Parks, John	39	do	do	do	
Rogers, M A	23	Ireland	Milwaukee, do	do	
Richardson, W H H	20	New York	New Lisbon do	Printer	Killed April 2d, 1865.
Rice, M H	42	Mass	Dayton, do	Farmer	
Rice, A D	18	do	do	do	Wounded in action, June 17, '64.

Name	Age	Birthplace	Residence	State	Occupation	Remarks
Russell, W W	18	Wisconsin	Fennimore,	Wis	Farmer	[Accidentally in left leg, April, [4th, '65. Leg amputated.
Sargeant, J M	32	N Hampshire	Clifton,	do	do	Promoted to Corporal, Sept, 1, 1864. Wounded April 2d, '65. Discharged June 22d 1865.
Smith, N W	20	New York	Onro,	do	do	Promoted to Corp'l July 1, '65.
Seymour, C H	18	Michigan	Peshtigo,	do	do	Promoted to Corp'l March 1, '65
Selleck, G A	38	Wisconsin	Waupaca,	do	do	Died in hospital Feb'y 18, 1865.
Smith, Wm A	19	Germany	Waupaca	do	do	Wounded in action June 17, '64.
Shannon, Nat	23	New York	Stockton	do	do	Wounded and taken prisoner July 30, 1864.
Sawyer, R D	16	Maine	Dayton	do	do	Promoted to Corp'l May 20, '65.
Smith, P B	34	Vermont	Little River	do	Mechanic	Discharged June 13, 1865.
Sherman, Horace	44	New York	Eldorado	do	Farmer	Wounded in action July 30, '64.
Stewart, Sam	18	Wisconsin	Fennimore	do	do	
Seymour, J S	18	do	Peshtigo	do	do	Wounded in action June 17, '64.
Thomas, F J	18	New York	Waupaca	do	do	Died June, 1864.
Tice, Jesse	19	Penn	Onro	do	do	Promoted to Corp'l, May 27, '65
Wilkins, A E	17	Vermont	Farmington, Wis		Farmer	Taken prisoner July 30, 1864, and exchanged. Discharged [May 19, 1865.
White, J W	21	New York	Royalton,	do	do	Discharged for disability.
Wolf, J A	44	Maine	Iola	do	do	
Whipple, Ira	44	New York	Farmington,	do	Musician	
Walker, Henry	17	Vermont	do	do	Farmer	
Weston, Edgar	21	do	Little Wolf	do	do	Wounded June 17, 1864. Died June 21, 1864.

RECRUITS.

Name	Age	Birthplace	Residence	State	Occupation	Remarks
Weiland, Henry	18	Wisconsin	Oshkosh,	do	do	Died July 26, 1864.
Balzer, August	37	Germany	Killaru Wis		Farmer	

COMPANY B.—[CONTINUED.]

NAMES.	AGE.	WHERE BORN.	RESIDENCE.	OCCUPATION.	REMARKS.
			RECRUITS.		
Bendikson, O	39	Norway	Mt. Morris, Wis	Farmer	
Bassett, David	43	Canada	Fall Village, Mass	do	
Clark, Thos	16	New York	Lomira, Wis	Laborer	
Church, D M	17	Wisconsin	N. Berlin, Wis	Farmer	
Dunbar, M V B	18	New York	Omro, do	do	
Ellikson, John	34	Norway	Mt Morris do	do	
Ewer, Esben	43	New York	Embarrass do		Wounded in action April 2, '65.
Font, Edward	30	Canada	Delafield, do	Shoemaker	[Discharged May 31, 1865.
Florence, Albert	21	do	F'd du Lac, do	Farmer	
Hintsman, A	41	Germany	Kildare, do	do	Wounded in action April 2, '65.
Halverson, Ole	38	Norway	Fountain, do	do	
Hobart, Charles	18	Wisconsin	Marathon Co., Wis	do	
Hibbard, Leander	25	Mass	Rosendale, do		Discharged May 29, 1865.
Johnston, W H	34	Connecticut	Avon, Wis	Farmer	Wounded in action April 2, '65.
Jarvis, James	39	Norway	Mt Morris do	do	[Discharged June 13, 1865.
Kremer, John	18	Germany	Oshkosh do	Laborer	
Kremer, M	18	Germany	Oshkosh, Wis	Laborer	
Martin, N S	23	New York	Utica, Wis	Farmer	
Martin, Richard	40	do	Richford Wis	do	
Peterson, J P	18	Norway	Oshkosh do	do	
Perkins, Harmon	26	Vermont	Amherst do	do	Dis. May 29, 1865.
Troup, Nelson	35	Ohio	Kildare do	do	
Weber, Leopold	29	Germany	do do	do	Dis. July 7, 1865
Weber, Peter	16	do	do do	do	Dis. June 9, 1865.

COMPANY C.—MUSTERED OUT JULY 25TH, 1865.

NAMES.	AGE.	WHERE BORN.	RESIDENCE.	OCCUPATION.	REMARKS.
SERGEANTS.					
1st H H Sleeper	26	New York	Berlin, Wis	Trader	Died a pris'r of war, Dec. 28, '64.
2d J D Million	25	Wisconsin		Farmer	Promoted 1st Serg't July 11, '64. Prom'td 2d Lieut. Nov. 14, '64.
3d Myron L Bowen	39	New York	Berlin, Wis	Butcher	Wounded July 23, 1864. Discharged Nov. 28, 1864.
4th A A Devore	39	Ohio	do	Saddler	Promoted to Ord'y Serg't Nov. 15, 1864.
5th Chas A Hawley	27	Illinois	Argyle, Wis	Farmer	Promoted to 2d Serg't Nov. 15, 1864. Dis. May 29, 1865.
CORPORALS.					
A J Hunter	23	Vermont	Kingston, Wis	Farmer	Promoted to Serg't March 18, '65
J M Paine	29	Maine	Argyle, do	Mechanic	Promoted to Serg't Nov. 15, '64. Wounded in wrist on picket line, Dec. 8, 1864. Dis. June 9th, 1865.
S K Little	33	New York	Aurora, Wis	Clergyman	Promoted to Serg't June 15, '65.
Alonzo Allen	36	Indiana	Argyle, Wis	Mason	Discharged Jan. 21, 1865.
Albert Oates	30	Wisconsin	Berlin do	Seaman	Transf'd to V R C Dec. 20, '64.
Q A Penniston	32	England	Argyle do	Farmer	Wounded in hand, June 17, '64. Promoted to Serg't Nov. 15, 1864.
G Evans	25	Wales	Berlin, Wis	do	Transf'd to V R C Feb. 22, '64.
G H Chapman	21	England	do	Saddler	Promoted to Serg't May 30, '65.

PRIVATES.

Name	Age	Nativity	Residence	Occupation	Remarks
Anderson, Eric	18	Norway	Argyle, Wis	Farmer	Discharged Jan. 25, 1865.
Arnold, D T	25	Penn	do	do	Detailed in Ambulance Corps, July, 1864.
Ashford, Wm	18	England	Berlin, Wis	do	Mustered out May 27, 1865.
Biesenthal, F	20	Germany	Princeton, Wis	Laborer	Reported as desert'd Nov. 19, '64.
Brown, Thos	23	Ireland	Argyle, do	Farmer	Died in Mount Pleasant hospital, Washington, D. C., Oct 30, '64, of consumption.
Blair, Henry	18	Penn	Darlington do	do	Died Emery's Hospital, Dec. 28, 1864, of chronic diarrhoea.
Butlington, A C	18	do	Argyle, do	do	Discharged Oct. 13, 1864, in Beverly Hospital, N. J.
Bruce, C J	25	New York	Berlin, Wis	Painter	Wounded, March 26, before [Petersburg.
Bradway, H A	22	do	Poysippi, do	Farmer	Discharged for disability, Jan'y 31, 1865.
Barr, Wm T	24	Ohio	Pine River, do	do	
Beulen, Robert	45	New York	Aurora, do	do	
Bunker, M F	18	Wisconsin	Pine River, do	Laborer	Died in 1st Div. 9th A C Hospital, May 22, 1865.
Botteker, Julius	18	Germany	Princeton, do	Farmer	Detailed in Amb.Corps July, '64.
Curey, H C	19	Ohio	Fayette, do	do	Wounded in action, June 17, '64.
Cline, A D	31	Penn	do, do	do	Died there from June 22.
Carleton, Henry	18	Wisconsin	Berlin, do	Clerk	Transferred to V R C, Dec.7, '64.
Chase, Chas E	19	Mass	do	Laborer	Promoted Corp. Feb. '65. W'd'd in action Petersb'g April 2, '65.
Cook, Chas H	18	New York	Pine River, do	do	Promoted to Corp. May 30, '65.
Carey, Benj A	44	Connecticut	do	Farmer	

Name	Age	Birthplace	Residence	State	Occupation	Remarks
Daniels, Leonard	44	New York	Berlin,	Wis	Farmer	Promoted to Corp. Feb'y, 1865.
Dilline, Albert	18	Ohio	Saxville	do	do	Promoted to Corp'l May 30, '05.
Erickson, Christian	19	Norway,	Argyle,	do	do	
Evans, Vernon	44	Ohio	Berlin	do	do	Dis. Dec. 23, '64, under age.
Evans, Wm	16	Wisconsin	do	do	do	
Fogel, John	38	Germany	Washington	do	do	
Forsyth, Edmund	16	Wisconsin	Berlin	do	do	
Gritznaker, C	26	Russia	Ripon,	do	Laborer	Died in Beverly Hospital, August 31, 1864.
Hess, Stephen G	23	New York	Rushford	do	Farmer	Wounded June 16, 1864, near Petersburg, Va. Died June 26, 1864, Washington, D. C.
Hanson, Nicholas	44	do	Aurora	do	Blacksmith	Wounded in both legs and breast, in action before Petersburg, Va., April 2d, 1865.
Harrington, D	24	Canada	Oregon	do	Farmer	Died July 11, 1864, of congestion of lungs.
Halleck, C Y	20	Penn	Princeton	do	Laborer	
Hicks, Robt	32	England	do	do	do	
Higgins, F M	25	Wisconsin	Kingston	do	Cooper	Promoted to Corp'l July 1864.
Huys, James F	22	New York	Buffalo,	do	Farmer	Wounded April 2, '65. Dis. May [24, 1868.
Jackson, Peter W	27	Indiana	Princeton,	do	do	Wounded severely June 17, '64. Discharged May 23, 4865.
Kelly, Nathan E	19	New York	Pine Lake	do	do	Promoted to Corp'l Feb'y 1865.
Karr, Jos	26	do	New Lisbon	do	do	Died Nov. 5, 1864, in Lincoln General Hospital.
Miliken, Jay F	18	Maine	Saxville	Wis	Farmer	Died Sept. 13, 1864, in Mower
Mosher, F E	22	Penn	Argyle	do	do	
Mosher, J D	18	Wisconsin	do	do	do	

COMPANY C.—[CONTINUED.]

NAMES.	AGE.	WHERE BORN.	RESIDENCE.	OCCUPATION.	REMARKS.
Oleson, Ole B	18	Norway	Walnut Spring, Wiota, Wis	Farmer	[Hospital, Phila.
Oleson, Henry	18	do	Wiota, Wis	do	Wounded June 17, 1864. Discharged June 17, 1865.
Olds, Ebenezer	31	New York	Oshkosh, Wis	do	Wounded on picket June 18, '64, and again the same month.
Perry, Geo W	21	Vermont	New Lisbon, Wis	do	
Perry, Alanson	21	Indiana	Korn	do	Slightly wounded Sept. 30, '64.
Perry, J R	33	Mass	Berlin	do	Dis. Dec. 19, '64. Left fore-arm amputated.
Proctor, Wm	39	England	Marion	do	Died Sept. 13, '64, in Alexandria
Parmalee, D B	42	Connecticut	Berlin	Laborer	Died en route to Washington, July 26, 1864.
Peterson, Hans	23	Denmark	Pine River	Farmer	
Penniston, D	27	England	Argyle	do	
Powell, John	18	New York	do	do	Transf'd to V. R. C. June 9, '65.
Piskery, J H	31	Germany	New Lisbon	Barber	Wounded in July, 1864, near Petersburg, and discharged April 8, 1865.
Rivers, Alfred	43	Canada East	Aurora	Farmer	Wounded June 17, 1864, and died July 6, 1864.
Reed, Warren	22	New York	Pine River	do	Died June 1, '64, at Washington, D. C.
Stevens, Wm H	18	do	Aurora	do	Died Sept. 28, 1864, at Washington, D. C.
Smith, J F	19	Vermont	Berlin	do	
Sherman, Charles	20	Ohio	New Lisbon	do	Mustered out May 26, 1865.

–

Name	Age	Born	Residence	State	Occupation	Remarks
Thompson, Thos G	20	Norway	Argyle		Farmer	Killed June 17, 1865.
Trousdale, Geo N	18	Wisconsin	Lafayette		do	Slightly wounded in head June 17, 1864. Promoted Corp'l Nov. 14, 1861.
Vanairsdale, T F	30	New York	Saxville,	do	do	Discharged, Sept 29, 1864.
Werner, August	18	Germany	Princeton,	do	Laborer	Discharged, Sept 2, 1864.
Whipple, Wm	44	New York	Aurora,	do	Cooper	
Williams, Israel	42	do	Rushford,	do	do	
Westenberg, Wm	34	Germany	Appleton,	do	Farmer	
Wood, Chas B	36	New York	Berlin,	do	Artist	
Wright, C B	18	do	Argyle,	do	Farmer	Dis. June 9, 1865.
Witchcraft, Wm	16	Wisconsin	Princeton,	do	do	
Wright, Geo C	16	do	Berlin,	do	do	
Willings, Victor	19	Prussia	Seneca,	do	Farmer	Drummer. Dis. June 9, 1865.

RECRUITS.

Name	Age	Born	Residence	State	Occupation	Remarks
Bullman, E C	18	Wisconsin	Bro'town,	Wis	Farmer	Dis. June 2, 1865.
Baldwin, Geo	37	New York	Stockbr'ge,	do	do	Dis. May 30, 1865.
Breed, John E	42	do	Enbarrass,	do	Physician	Dis. do 27, 1865.
Bintliff, Gershom,	34	England	Monroe	do	Farmer	
Chase, Nathan O	42	Maine	Seneca,	do	do	
Coghis, John B	39	New York,	Broth'to'n	do	do	Dis. June 2, 1865.
Gondeman, Geo A	16	do	Winneconne,	do	do	Killed April 2, 1865.
Collins, Hugh,	34	Ireland.			Laborer	Dis. Camp Randall, Sep. 22, '64.
Davids, Daniel	24	Wisconsin,	Stockbridge,	do	Farmer	Dis. June 30, 1865.
Fowler, Jas D	24	do	Bro'town,	do	do	Dis. do 2, 1865.
Fitzgibbon, Jas	28	Canada			Laborer	Wound'd March 31, '65, on picket.
Kinnes, Jas H	26	New York	Bro'town,	do	Farmer	Des. Camp Randall, Sept. 2, '64.
Niles, Solomon	25	Wisconsin	do	do	do	Discharged June 2, 1865. do do 2, do

COMPANY C.—[CONTINUED.]

NAMES.	AGE.	WHERE BORN.	RESIDENCE.	OCCUPATION.	REMARKS.
Pendleton, John	27	New York	Stockbr'ge, Wis	Farmer	Discharged Jan. 5, 1865.
Sears, John,	37	New York	do do	do	do June 2, do
Taylor, W H	29	Wisconsin	Winnebago Co	Musician	do do 6, do
Welch, Chas	30	New York	Brothertown, Wis	Farmer	do do 2, do
Welch, Hira	43	do	Stockbridge do	do	do do 2, do
Welch, S	23	do	do do	do	Wounded in leg Oct. 8, 1864.
					Discharged June 2, 1865.
Welch, Cyrus	19	Wisconsin	do do	do	Discharged June 14, 1865.
Welch, Lewis	29	New York	do do	do	do do 2, do
Wilmarth, A W	32	Mass	Embarrass do	do	do do 2, do

COMPANY D.—MUSTERED OUT JULY 25TH, 1865.

NAMES.	AGE.	WHERE BORN.	RESIDENCE.		OCCUPATION.	REMARKS.
SERGEANTS.						
1st ChaunceyW Hyatt	26	New York	Hingham,	Wis	Teacher	Discharged Dec. 23, 1864, and promoted to 2d Lieut.
2d John J Coyle	37	Ireland	Avoca,	do	Blacksmith	Promoted 1st Serg't Jan. 1, '65. Promoted 2d Lieut., 52d Reg't, March 15, 1865.
3d Ben L Hoylands	36	Ohio	Monroe	do	Farmer	Discharged per order War Dept, March 29, 1865.
4th T S Winchell	21	Wisconsin	Plainville	do	Lumberman	Discharged to accept commission of 2d Lieut. in 50th Reg't, March 29, 1865.
5th Franklin Glover	18	Penn	Monroe	do	Student	Transferred, and promoted 1st Serg't, Co. F, Dec. 1, 1864.
CORPORALS.						
Franklin Wilcox	23	Ohio	Lemonwier	do	Soldier	Promoted Serg't Jan. 1, 1865. [Promoted 1st Sergt March 15, 1865.
Edward B Hartson	26	Illinois	N Chester	do	Farmer	Wounded June 17, 1864. Promoted Serg't Jan. 1, 1865. Mortally wounded April 2, 1865. Died April 18, 1865.
John Wyatt	32	do	Monroe	do	do	
Lee Ballou	33	New York	do	do	do	Wounded November 23, 1864.

COMPANY D.—[CONTINUED.]

NAMES.	AGE.	WHERE BORN.	RESIDENCE.	OCCUPATION.	REMARKS.
Pat H McCarthy	18	Canada	Richland Wis	Teacher	Sent to hospital in July, 1864.
James B Barnes	23	Ohio	Reedsburg do	Farmer	[Discharged May 26, 1865.
Findley Snyder	21	Indiana	Richland do	Teacher	Died May 12, '64, Baltimore, Md.
John S Stephenson	36	Penn	Monroe do	Farmer	Wounded June 17, 1864. Died
			PRIVATES.		
Abbott, Richard S	24	N Brunswick	Manitowoc da	Teacher do *[handwritten]*	[July, 1864.
Arndt, Frederick	18	Prussia	Princeton do	do	Wounded by sharpshooter, Oct., 1864; also, April 24, 1865. Discharged May 29, 1865.
Austin, Alfred E	23	Canada	Waupun do	do	Wounded June 17, 1864. Promoted Corporal April 1, '65.
Andrews, John S	18	Mass	Monroe do	do *[handwritten]*	Appointed Corporal, May 12, 1864. Wounded Aug. 13, '64.
Buzzell, Soldern P	21	do	NewLisbon do	do	Leg amputated. Discharged Jan. 14, 1865.
Burgess, Wingit	39	Maine	Hingham, Wis	Mechanic	Drummer and nurse in hospital.
Brigham, Jas J	37	Mass	Pilot Knob, do	Farmer	Dis. for disability Sept. 25, 1861.
Belleville, C D	40	Ohio	Richl'd Centre do	Surveyor	Dis. for disability Sept. 23, 1864.
Bowers, Alfred	39	do	Excelsior do	Farmer *[handwritten]*	
Bradley, N G	19	New York	Tomah do	do *[handwritten]*	Discharged May 24, 1865.
Brown, J K P	20	Penn	Monroe do	do	
Barton,	23	Prussia	Princeton do	Shoemaker *[handwritten]*	
Barton, Wm F	20	Ohio		Farmer	
Clemmer, Jac	27	Penn	Monroe	do	Wounded June 17, 1864.

Name	Age				Occupation	Remarks
Chambers, J M	22	Illinois	do	do	Merchant	Promoted Com. Sergt. April 15, 1864.
Clinard, August	30	Prussia	Princeton	do	Laborer	Wounded June 17, 1864. Discharged Feb. 6, 1865.
Campbell, D D	20	New York	Oxford	do	Farmer	Wounded June 17, 1864. Never returned to regiment.
Carr, Amos	44	do	Darlington	do	do	Died at Washington Oct. 1, 1864.
Carter, N B	37	Maine	Casey's Tav'n	do	do	Wounded June 17, 1863. Never returned.
Carr, J R	25	Illinois	Darlington	do	do	
Dotch, Jno	20	Ohio	Sheboygan	do	Cooper	
Dresser, A	38	Canada	Brandon	do	Farmer	Promoted to Corp. April 1, 1865.
Duncars, Thos	43	Penn	Monroe	do	Carpenter	
French, L S	18	Wisconsin	Hingham	do	Farmer	Promoted Corp. June 2, 1865.
Foster, Harrison	30	Ohio	New Chester	do	do	
Faulkner, Thos	18	New York	Tomah	do	do	Died from wounds rec'd June 17, 1864, before Petersburg.
Feather, Jeff	26	Penn	Monroe,	do	do	Promoted Corporal April 1, 1865.
Frankenberger,	25	Penn	Monroe,	do	Teacher	
Giles, Fish,	16	Upper Canada	Avoca,	do	Farmer	Drummer.
Grace, Wm J	18	England,	Monroe,	do	Blacksmith	
Godfrey, John D	37	Canada,	Millard,	do	Farmer	
Gibson, R W	26	New Jersey	Pilot Knob,	do	Lumberman	
Green, Thos	34	Ireland	Fond du Lac	do	do	
Holden, J Jr	37	Connecticut	Lavalle	do	Farmer	
Huskins, C A	24	New York	Oxford	do	do	Accidentally wounded in foot, Jan 1865. Promoted Corp'l [June 2] 1865.
Hoadley, Thos	23	do	Pilot Knob	do	do	
Hart, J M	33	Kentucky	Waupun	do	do	
Hundt, Peter	17	Prussia	Princeton	do	do	Discharged June 12, 1865.

COMPANY D.—[CONTINUED.]

NAMES.	AGE.	WHERE BORN.	RESIDENCE.	Wis	OCCUPATION.	REMARKS.
Hyde, Thos	31	England	Lavalle	Wis	Farmer	Detailed and served as Clerk for Assistant A. Q. M. Transf'd to V. R. C. April 1, '65.
Irwin, Edward	27	Nova Scotia	Waupun	do	Blacksmith	
Johnson, B K	36	Vermont	Fayette	do	Farmer—	
Johnson, John	36	Norway	North Cape	do	Shoemaker	Discharged June 17, 1865.
Long, Abner	41	New York	Monroe	do	Farmer—	Discharged June 2, 1865.
Keith, M	43	do		do	do	
Kendall, S	20	do	Avoca	do	do	Promoted Corp. March 15, 1865.
Martz, Wm	34	Ohio	Waterloo	do	do	Died in Washington, Oct., 1865.
Mason, C Y	41	Vermont	Hingham	do	Shoemaker	Wounded June 20, 1864. Dis. [June 16, 1865.
Matison, J	28	Norway	Norway	do	Farmer	Drummer.
Mason, C D	16	Ohio	Hingham	do	Shoemaker	
Notman, D	24	Scotland	Avoca	do	Farmer—	Promoted Corp. June, 1864, and Serg't April 1865.
Parks, Franklin	25	Mass	Waterloo	do	Cooper	Killed at Cold Harbor, June 12, 1864.
Osborne, G W	27	Penn	Pilot Knob	do	Farmer	Died of chronic diarrhœa, in [Mount Pleasant Hospital, August 10, 1864.
Phillips, G	42	New York	Monroe	do	do	
Pierce, Joseph M	39	do	do	do	Merchant	Promoted to Corporal, May '61.
Randall, Jacob	16	Wisconsin	do	do	Farmer—	Dis. for disability, Jan. 20, 1865.
Rule, T B	37	Penn	Fayette	do	do	Dis. for disability March 2, 1865.
Raynes, J J	23	England	Danville	do	do	
Roller, Jos	18	Germany	New Chester	do	Farmer—	Killed on picket line, Jan. 8, 65.
Risden, Geo	29	England	Mauston	do	do	

Name	Age	Nativity	Residence	Wis	Occupation	Remarks
Tasker, D	.					
Temple, Justin	18	Prussia	Princeton	Wis	Farmer	Served with R. Q. M.
Vall, H S	24	Mass	Philaville	do	do	Appointed Corporal July 10, '64, [and as Serg't April 1, 1865.
Vaughn G B	17	Wisconsin	Avoca	do	do	
Whitford, Wm H	28	Ohio		do	do	
Williamson, R	21	Wisconsin	Mineral Point	do	do	
Woodman, J H	27	Scotland	Tomah	do	do	
Wing, Andrew	18	Missouri	Monroe	do	Printer	
Squires, J W	31	New York	New Chester	do	Carpenter	
	38	do	Sheboygan	do	Cooper	Wounded June 13, 1864. Died June 28, 1864.
Smith, James	20	Illinois	Elmira	do	Farmer	Discharged June 13, 1865.
Spaulding, B	28	Mass	Oxford	do	do	Promoted Corporal June 2, 1865.
Steve, W D	16	Wisconsin	Fond du Lac	do	Laborer	
Swenie, Levi	23	Virginia	Tampico	do	Farmer	
Sisley, M	18	Prussia	Princeton	do	do	
Sammon, A	22	do	do	do	Butcher	Promoted Corporal May 27, '65.

RECRUITS.

Name	Age	Nativity	Residence	Wis	Occupation	Remarks
Bell, John S	26	Penn	Monroe	do	Farmer	Discharged June 2, 1865.
Baker, A M	18	Wisconsin	do	do	do	Discharged June 2, 1865.
Caughey, Thos L	23	Penn	do	do	do	Wounded April 2, 1865, at Fort Mahone. Dis. June 15, 1865.
Chapman, Benj F	38	New York	do	do	do	Discharged June 2, 1865.
Frankenberger, H	25	Penn	do	do	Teacher	Promoted Corporal April 1, 1865. Discharged June 2, 1865.
Hammond, A	35	Indiana	do	do	Farmer	Promoted Corporal Jan. '65, and to Serg't April, '65. Dis. June 2, 1865.
Griffith, T	22	Penn	do	do	do	Discharged June 2, 1865.

COMPANY D.—[CONTINUED.]

NAMES.	AGE.	WHERE BORN.	RESIDENCE.	OCCUPATION.	REMARKS.
Gist, George V	19	Wisconsin	Monroe, Wis	Farmer	Discharged June 2, 1865.
McCracken, J W	31	Illinois	do	do	Detailed in Pioneer Corps. Dis. June 2, 1865.
Nobles, George J	44	New York	do	do	Detailed in Pioneer Corps. Dis. June 2, 1865.
Pierce, Jos M	30	do	do	Merchant	Promoted to Corp. May, 1865. Dis. June 2, 1865.
Smith, George	44	England	do	Farmer	Discharged June 2, 1865.
Wallace, D	29	Illinois	do	do	do do 2, do
Walker, J M	41	Penn	do	Minister	Discharged and appointed Chaplain, Oct. 19, '65.

COMPANY E.—MUSTERED OUT JULY 25TH, 1865.

NAMES.	AGE.	WHERE BORN.	RESIDENCE.	OCCUPATION.	REMARKS.
SERGEANTS.					
1st Chas A Smith	26	Ohio	New Lisbon, Wis	Book-keeper	Wounded July 30, 1864. Died Sept. 22, 1864.
2d O A Benedict	27	do	Waupaca	do	Farmer	Promoted 1st Serg't July 6, '65. Dis. July 27, 1865
3d E A Bentley	34	New York	Princeton	do	do	Promoted to 1st Serg't Oct. 1st, 1864. Commissioned 2d Lieut. Nov. 12th, 1864.
4th H A Gardiner	30	do	Mosinee	do	Landlord	Killed August 21st, 1864.
5th Ashley Smith	39	do	New Lisbon	do	Farmer	
CORPORALS.					
Wm McKay	40	Ireland	do	do	Carpenter & Joiner	Promoted Serg't Sept. 1st, 1864.
Jno E Wess	19	Germany	Palmyra	do	Farmer	Wounded July 29th 1864.
Jno K Allen	32	Mass	New Lisbon	do	do	Wounded Aug. 8, '64. Transferred to V R Corps Jan. 8th, 65.
J Cornish	27	New York	Germantown	do	.	Wounded July 30th, 1864 Dis. May 19th, 1865.
Thomas Dolan	24	Canada	Mosinee	do	Lumberman	Promoted to 5th Serg't June 28, 1865.
John Cumpen	21	Michigan	Detroit, Michigan	Farmer	Deserted June 26th, 1864.
E Erickson	20	Wisconsin	Palmyra, Wis	do	Promoted Serg't Nov. 12th, '64; to 1st Serg't July 28, 1865.

COMPANY E.—[CONTINUED.]

NAMES.	AGE.	WHERE BORN.	RESIDENCE.	OCCUPATION.	REMARKS.
H Wadsworth	37	Penn	New Lisbon, Wis	Shoemaker	Taken prisoner July 30, 1864, and afterwards paroled. Dis. May 20, 1865.
PRIVATES.					
Abbey, Francis	18	E Canada	Fond du Lac, Wis	Farmer	
Bostwick, A E	18	Vermont	Waupaca do	do	Wounded Aug. 21, 1864.
Boseski, M F	26	Germany	Milwaukee do	Laborer	
Brink, L	22	Illinois		Farmer	Deserted June 15th, 1864.
Blandon, C J	18	New York	Sheldon, Minn	do	
Carpenter, A	26	Michigan	New Lisbon, Wis	do	Promoted to Corp. June 6, '65.
Cariker, H W	35	N Carolina	Hillsbrough, Ill	do	Killed Aug. 21, 1864.
Clews, John	24	England	New Lisbon, Wis	do	Discharged.
Carter, Jac	44	New York	Waupun do	do	Wounded Aug. 10, 1864. Discharged March 18, 1865.
Connor, Edw	19	Wisconsin	Wausau do	Lumberman	Wounded July 30, 1864, and April 2d, 1865. Dis. May 26, 1865.
Cass, Asa	27	Canada	Oconto do	Farmer	Discharged Feb'y 4, 1865, by Special Order War Dep't.
Cook, R	18	New York	Omro do	do	Deserted June 15, 1864.
Canada, M	25	Ireland	Marinette do	Laborer	
Coon, Henry	18	Wisconsin	Milwaukee do	Student	
Dubay, Moses	18	Wisconsin	Wausau do	Trapper	
Dechadieu, M	20	do	do	Laborer	Wounded July 30, 1864. Dis. for disability Dec. 5, 1864.

Name	Age	Nativity	Residence	State	Occupation	Remarks
Dechurdieu, J	21	Wisconsin	Wausau	Wis	Lumberman	Wounded Aug. 21, 1864. Discharged April 27, 1865.
Drake, Robert	18	New York	Ripon	do	Farmer	Promoted to Corp. June 6, '65.
Daniels, L A	18	Ohio	Germantown	do	Lumberman	Discharged March, 1865, to accept commission.
Dean, Jno	44	Vermont	Milwaukee	do	Lawyer	
Forbes, Joel	38	Conn	New Lisbon	do	Farmer	Wounded and taken prisoner [July 30, 1864.
Friesbourg, H H	33	Norway	Madison	do	do	
Flynn, E C	42	New York	Milwaukee	do	Mason	
Fogle, Abraham	26	Penn	Fond du Lac	do	Cooper	
Guyott, Boswell	18	Wisconsin	Wausau	do	Hunter	Wounded April 2, 1865.
Gerard, Samuel	45	New York	Oshkosh	do	Lumberman	Discharged June 7, 1865.
George, Ed	18	Wales	New Lisbon	do	Farmer	Discharged May 19, 1865.
Harp, Wm	18	Prussia	Milwaukee	do	Watchmaker	Deserted June 15, 1864.
Hartwick, W	27	do	Ripon	do	Teacher	Taken prisoner July 30, 1864, and paroled.
Holton, J H	19	Ireland	Deerfield	do	Farmer	Deserted July 12, 1864, from Camp Randall, Wis.
Hallowell, J K	18	Canada	Fond du Lac, Wis		Clerk	Wounded July 30, 1864. Appointed Corporal July 4th, '64; promoted to Serg't Oct. 1, '64; promoted to 1st Serg't Nov. 12th, 1864; wounded April 2, '65. Dis. June 6, 1865.
House, Elijah	19	New York	Hancock	do	Farmer	
Hill, W F	22	Vermont	New Lisbon	do	do	Died in General Hospital, 9th A. C., Sept. 17th, 1864.
Joslin, T P	33	do	Palmyra	do	Carpenter	Appointed Corporal Oct. 1st, '61. Wounded April 2, 1865.
Johnson, Wm L	18	Iowa	Milwaukee	do	Artist	Killed July 30th, 1864.

COMPANY E.—[Continued.]

NAMES.	AGE.	WHERE BORN.	RESIDENCE.	OCCUPATION.	REMARKS.
Koethe, J	18	Germany	Hokah, Minn	Farmer	Promoted Corp. June 6, 1865.
Keefe, J Jr	21	New York	Mosinee, Wis	Laborer	do do do 6, do
Lawrence, O	23	Norway	New Lisbon, Wis	Farmer	Wounded August 21st, 1864,
Lunn, Andrew	33	Sweden	Peshtigo do	Sailor	Transferred to U. S. Navy, July 11th, 1864.
Misler, A	44	France	Packwaukee do	Farmer	Killed April 2, 1865.
Miller, Jno	42	Germany	New Lisbon do	Laborer	Deserted from Camp Randall, July 19th, 1864.
Monger, C A	19	Ohio	Boltonville do	Farmer	Died of heart disease Oct. 3, '64.
Mitchell, P	18	France	Mosinee do	Laborer	Appointed Corp. Sept. 1, '64; 4th Sergt, June 6, 1865.
Norton, H B	18	Wisconsin	New Lisbon do	Farmer	Appointed Corp. March 1, 1865.
Neal, P H	19	England	Packwaukee do	do	
Nelson, Lars	41	Norway	Milwaukee do	do	Wounded Sep. 30, 1864. Discharged Feb. 20, 1865.
Olenbroner, J	18	Germany	do do	Laborer	
Phillips, Ed	18	New York	Grandville do	do	
Rowland, J A	22	Vermont	New Lisbon do	Farmer	Wounded Aug. 7, 1864. Discharged May 29, 1865.
Redman, H	16	Michigan	Hancock do	do	
Roman, Chas	20	Germany	New Lisbon do	Laborer	
Rogers, Jas	21	Ireland	Milwaukee do	Tailor	
Row, Wm	21	New York	do do	Miller	Deserted from Camp Randall, June 4, 1864.
Scott, Joseph	20	Wisconsin	Mosinee do	Laborer	Deserted from Camp Randall, June 15, 1864. Wounded Sept. 30, 1864

Name	Age	Born	Residence	Occupation	Remarks
Stone, S F	18	do	Yucatan	Minn Farmer	Wounded Aug. 21, '64, and died.
Sienke, G	21	Germany	Hokah	do	Promoted Corporal June 6, '65.
Smith, F	18	do	Minnesota	do	
Sauers, A	19	Germany	Hokah, Minn	Farmer	Died of Typhoid fever, Sept. 16, 1864.
Stanley, J	19	N Carolina	Fond du Lac, Wis	do	Transferred to the Navy July 11th, 1864.
Stickney, Chas	80	New York	Peshtigo	Lumberman	Killed July 30th, 1864.
Skesue, S	42	do	Fond du Lac do	Farmer	Died in hospital Oct. 18, 1864.
Taylor, Henry	35	England	New Lisbon do	do	
Thompson, Wm	18	Penn	Milwaukee do	Cooper	
Webster, J	33	N Humpshire	New Lisbon do	Farmer	
Wilcox, J	23	Illinois	Marathon Co do	Laborer	
Wiegand, Wm	18	Germany	Hokah, Minn	Farmer	Missing in action of August 19, [1864.
Wess, Wm	18	do	Palmyra, Wis	do	
James, Mat ('	24	Virginia	St Louis, Mo	Cook, colored	

RECRUITS.

Name	Age	Born	Residence	Occupation	Remarks
Abbey, Orin	18	Canada	Fond du Lac, Wis	Laborer	Die June 2, 1865.
Booth, S M	24	do	Packwaukee, do	Laborer	
Brant, Samuel	19	Indiana	Spring Grove do	Farmer	
Bonnell, D T	18	New Jersey	Point Bluff do	do	
Caldwell, S B	38	Penn	Pedee do	Driver	Dis. June 2, 1865.
Churchill, C	33	Norway	Palmyra do	Farmer	do 2, do
Criswell, Thos	28	Penn	Tyrone, Penn	Sawyer	Wounded April 2, 1865. Discharged May 26, 1865.
Donges, John	36	Germany	Pedee, Wis	Farmer	Wounded April 2d, 1865, and died of wounds April 20, '65.
Gill, Fred O	18	Penn	Spring Grove, Wis	do	Discharged June 2, 1865.

COMPANY E.—[CONTINUED.]

NAMES.	AGE.	WHERE BORN.	RESIDENCE.	OCCUPATION.	REMARKS.
Holmes, H P	40	New York	New Lisbon, Wis	Farmer	Promoted to Corp. Nov. 12, '64. [Dis. June 2, 1865.]
Ingelbrecptein, L	19	Norway	Newark do	do	
Kishkobonish, L	20	Wisconsin	Green Bay do	do	
Kishkobonish, M	25	do	do	do	
Kline, I J	23	do	Spring Grove do	do	Dis. July 7, 1865.
Killer, Jac	20	Penn	Spring Grove do	Farmer	Dis. June 2, 1865.
Kilwine, P W	19	Germany	do	do	do 2, do
Leach, J P	16	Wisconsin		do	Dis. May 15, do
Newcomer, Geo	43	Penn	Pedee	do	Died in hospital Jan. 13, 1865.
Newcomer, Jos	16	Ohio	do	do	
Rowe, S F	29	Maine	Berlin	Carpenter	Dis. June 2, 1865.
Race, Chas	18	Germany	Milwaukee do	Laborer	do 2, do
Sauers, F W	22	Penn	Hokah, Minn	Farmer	Killed April 2, 1865.
Stearns, E D	41	New York	Orange, Wis	do	Dis. June 2, 1865.
Young, Geo C	22	do	Berlin do	Cooper	

COMPANY F.—MUSTERED OUT JULY 25TH, 1865.

NAMES.	AGE.	WHERE BORN.	RESIDENCE.		OCCUPATION.	REMARKS.
SERGEANTS.						
1st Henry Chase	37	Scotland			Moulder	Deserted at Chicago, Ill., Sept. 23, 1864.
2d F Thayer	19	Wisconsin	Palmyra	Wis	Farmer	Appointed Color Bearer.
3d John C Ford	32	Ireland	Milwaukee	do	Teacher	Reduced to the ranks, and promoted Corp. Dec. 1, 1864.
4th Charles Miller	33	Germany			Clerk	Promoted Serg't Maj. April 27, '65.
5th L M Bigelow	22	Vermont	Palmyra	do	Mechanic	Discharged Dec. 14, 1864.
CORPORALS.						
Corey Moin	26	Canada			Farmer	Reduced to the ranks Nov. 1, '64. Discharged June 19, 1865.
J H Porter	18	Wisconsin	Palmyra	Wis	do	Promoted Serg't Nov. 1, 1864.
D W Compton	26	New York	Grand Rapids	do	do	Promoted Serg't Dec. 1, 1864.
W H Monger	18	Wisconsin	Palmyra	do	do	
R A Lawrence	23	Illinois	Wauzeka	do	do	Wounded April 2, 1865. Discharged June 24, 1865.
M P Webb	25	Penn	Whitewater	do	Musician	Reduced to the ranks May 10, 1865. Discharged June 2, '65.
A H Trader	21	Illinois	Quincy	Ill	Harness-maker	Promoted Serg't Dec. 1, 1864.
A A Duffy	33	New York	Auburn	Wis	Mechanic	

COMPANY F.—[CONTINUED.]

PRIVATES.

NAMES.	AGE.	WHERE BORN.	RESIDENCE.	OCCUPATION.	REMARKS.
Aretush, Frank	21	Wisconsin	N. Wisconsin	Trapper	Chippewa Indian. Killed, April [2, 1865.
Bangemann, H	23	Germany	Menomonee, Wis	Carpenter	Menominee Indian, promoted Corp. June 4, 1865.
Boyd, Alfred	19	Wisconsin	Keshena, do	Laborer	
Brazee, S M	18	New York	Beechwood, do	Farmer	Accidentally wounded, Dec., '64.
Brennan, Jas	33	Ireland	Sparta, do	do	
Buck, George	18	New York		do	
Checkezick, K	21	Wisconsin	N. Wisconsin	Trapper	Chippewa Indian.
Clapp, H I	18	do	Berlin, Wis	Laborer	
McCarty, Thos	18	Mass	Forrest, do	Farmer	
Colburn, A	18	N. Hampshire	Spencerbr'k, Minn	do	
Collins, A	20	New York	McHenry, Ill	Mechanic	Little finger of left hand shot off Oct. 8. 1864. Left hand badly wounded Jan. 3, 1865. Amputated.
Castello, Thos	21	Ireland		Farmer	Deserted at Madison, Wis. in Sept., 1864.
Curr, Michael	22	do		Sailor	Deserted at Madison, Wis., in Sept., 1864.
Causwauac, M	27	Wisconsin	Oconto, Wis	Hunter	Indian, transferred from Co. G, [June 2, 1865.
Darrow, Richard	18	New York	Shawano, do	Mechanic	Wounded April 2, 1865. Dis. June 19, 1865.
Dowd, Jack	21	Wisconsin	Northern, do	Trapper	

Name	Age	Nativity	Residence	Occupation	Remarks
Dwyer, John	19	Ireland	New Lisbon do	Laborer	Killed April 2, 1865.
Desjardin, E	18	Canada	Cono, Canada E	Laborer	Deserted at Madison, Wis., in Aug. 1864.
Dile, Max	18	Bohemia	Milwaukee, Wis	Shoemaker	Promoted to Corp. Nov. 1864.
Duncan, J R	26	Canada		Wagon-maker	
Ellis, H H	19	Illinois	Whitewater, Wis	Cooper	Promoted 1st Sergt. Dec. 1, '64. Menominee Indian.
George, J W	32	Indiana	Columbus do	Laborer	Transferred from Co. G, June 2, 1865, and discharged June 26, '65. Promoted to Corp. May [13], 1865.
Glover, Frank	18	Penn	Monroe do	Student	
Greenlay, J	40	Wisconsin	Keshena do	Laborer	
Gardner, I	37	Canada	Pensaukee do	do	
Hunt, Job	29	Canada	Chicago, Illinois	Saloon keeper	Deserted at Madison, Wis., in [August, 1864.
Hackett, Wm	19	Ireland	Oconto Wis	Laborer	Discharged June 2, 1865.
Henry, Peter	26	do	Charleston do	Teamster	do do 2, do
Hammer, Geo	23	New York	Cold Spring do	Farmer	
Henderson, W A	30	Canada	Saxville do	do	Killed April 2, 1865. Menominee Indian.
James, Thos	28	Wales	Keshena do	do	
Jack, Indian	24	Wisconsin	Palmyra do	Hunter	
Johnson, J H	19	do	Stockbridge do	Farmer	Deserted Sept. 30, 1864. Returned to duty May 20, 1865.
Johnson, R	23	do		Laborer	Chippewa Indian
Ka-Ka-Sha	38	do	Linwood	Hunter	
Kittridge, C	25	Canada	Chicago, Illinois	Merchant	
Kuh-Keh-Mahot J	18	Wisconsin	Keshena Wis	Laborer	Menominee Indian. Wounded on picket Jan. 1, 1865. Discharged June 2, 1865.
Killina, Jno	25	Ireland		do	Deserted at Madison, Wis., in Sept. 1864.

COMPANY F.—[CONTINUED.]

NAMES.	AGE.	WHERE BORN.	RESIDENCE.		OCCUPATION.	REMARKS.
Kinney, L	21	Wisconsin	Keshena	Wis	Laborer	Menominee Indian.
Kolb, E	19	Germany	Berlin	do	Farmer	
Kauer, H	42	do	Fountain City	do	Laborer	Died in hospital Dec. 24, 1864.
Klauer, Jno	36	do	La Crosse	do	Laborer	
Lemar, William	20	Indiana	Marietta	Ind	Farmer	
Leonard, Peter	44	Ireland	Moscow	Wis	do	
Lindsay, Thos	22	New York			do	Desert'd Madison, Wis, Sept. '64.
Linke, B	18	Wisconsin	Palmyra	do	do	do do do do
Longfield, A	18	do	Cottage Grove	do	do	
Lafferty, James	28	Ireland		do	Sailor	do do do do
Mathews, R C	18	Ohio	Mayville	do	Farmer	
Marks, Wm	18	Conn	Wayanwega	do	do	
Martin, S	18	New York	Madison	do	do	
McCabe, J E	18	New Jersey	Eagle	do	do	
McDonnell, A	40	Hudson Bay	Peshtigo	do	Laborer	
Maska, G	35	Wisconsin	Linwood	do	Trapper	Chippewa Indian. Wound'd thro' left lung Dec. 13, '64, and died next day.
McCarthy, J	25	Ireland			Laborer	Deserted Madison, Wis.Sept.'64.
McDonough, M	35	do	Westport	do	Farmer	Wounded April 2, 1865. Discharged June 2, 1865.
Pierce, Amos	19	New Jersey	Franklin	N J	Lumberman	Promoted Corporal May 10, '65.
Pierce, Joseph	21	do do	do	do	do	
Peaches, N	28	Wisconsin	Red River	Wis	Farmer	Menominee Indian. Wounded and died June 31, 1861.

Name	Age	Nativity	Residence	Occupation	Remarks
Pjetchicote, P	20	do	Kewanee, Wis	Laborer	Transf'd from Co. G, June 2, '65
Ryan, M F	18	Vermont	Milwaukee, do	Sailor	Promoted Corp. June 26, 1865.
Riley, W F	18	Ohio	Vernon, do	Gunsmith	Musician.
Rounds, C E	18	Wisconsin	Palmyra, do	Farmer	Sick, and never left the State.
Ruhnke, C	44	Prussia	Milwaukee, do	Laborer	
Sawyer, H	18	Germany	Fond du Lac, do	Farmer	
Scott, Jos	24	Wisconsin	do	Laborer	Chippewa Indian. Wounded in head and died Jan. 8, 1865.
Scott, Jno	21	do	Linnwood, do	Hunter	Chippewa Indian.
Sullivan, T	31	Maryland		Laborer	Deserted at Madison, Wis, in September, 1864.
Schmidt, A	21	Germany		Laborer	Deserted at Madison, Wis, in August, 1864.
Steele, Ray	20	Wisconsin	New Berlin, Wis	Lumberman,	Promoted to Corp'l, Nov. 1864.
Smith, C J	19	New York	Palmyra, do	Laborer	[Discharged June 2, 1865.
Smith, Irwin	18	Penn	Spring Grove, do	Farmer	Discharged June 2, 1865.
Truax, Chas	18	New York	Mosinee, do	Laborer	Killed April 2, 1865.
Williams, Jas	27	Wisconsin	Keshena, do	Hunter	Menominee Indian.
Wilson, Henry	28	Michigan	Muskegon, Mhn	Engineer	Promoted to Corporal Dec. '64.
Wilson, Geo	22	Canada		Gardener	Deserted at Madison, Wis, in Sept. 1864.
White, J	19	England	Milwaukee, Wis	Sailor	Transferred from Co. G, June 2, 1865.
Yore, Benj	44	Germany	Cataract do	Laborer	Discharged May 29, 1865.

COMPANY G.—MUSTERED OUT JULY 25TH, 1865.

NAMES.	AGE.	WHERE BORN.	RESIDENCE.	OCCUPATION.	REMARKS.
SERGEANTS.					
1st Chas H Marsh	22	Ohio	Lima Center, Wis	Farmer	
2d J W Eggleston	29	New York	Albion	Blacksmith	
3d F L Whitney	31	do	Pensaukee	Farmer	
4th C C Birum	22	Norway	Baraboo	do	Wounded April 2d, 1865.
5th M D Delano	38	New York	Pensaukee	do	
CORPORALS.					
Fred, W John	37	Prussia	Steles,	Wis	Lumberman	Promoted to 5th Sergt Feb'y 20, 1865.
L W Hardwick	22	Wisconsin	Pensaukee	do	do	Reduced to the ranks Nov. 24, 1864. Re-appointed Corporal Feb'y 20, 1865. Wounded [April 2, 1865.
F B Anderson	21	New York	Lima Centre	do	Farmer	Wounded April 2d, 1865.
L W Sherman	24	do	Edgerton,	do	do	Killed by a shell, Feb'y 16th '65.
William Dunn	30	England	Albion	do	do	Wounded Dec. 13th, 1864.
G A Warren	22	Penn	Lima Centre	do	do	
Benj F Compton	28	New York	Stoughton	do	do	
J C Barnes	29	Wisconsin	Albion	do	do	
PRIVATES.					
Atley, John	21	Pennsylvania	Cross Plains	Wis	Farmer	
Atkin, Peter	18	England			do	Des. at Camp Randall. Sep.18, '64

Name	Age	Birthplace	Residence	Wis	Occupation	Remarks
Butts, Jac	29	Pennsylvania	Dunkirk	Wis	Farmer	Des. at Camp Randall, Sep. 18, '64
Boss, J W	33	New York	Albion	do	do	Died at 9th A. C. Hospital, City Point, Va., Feb. 19, '65, of acute rheumatism.
Barton, Thomas	20	England	Milford	do	do	Wounded April 2, '65. Died in Hospital at Alexandria.
Brown, Wm	37	Germany				Des. at Washington, Sep 27, '64.
Beyer, A	19	Prussia	Milford	do	do	Died in General Hospital, Madison, Oct. 2, 1864.
Braidy, Charles	23	Ohio	Iowa City	Iowa	do	
Both, Charles	22	Hamburg	do	do	Engineer	
Camp, S J	29	Ohio	Koshkonong	Wis	Farmer	
Courtright, A	24	New York	Albion	do	do	
Compton, J G	33	do	Dunkirk	do	do	
Conradt, I	23	do	do	do	do	
Cannon, E D	37	do	do	do	do	
Cook, Joseph	27	England	Edgerton	do	do	Wounded April 2, 1865.
Campbell, M	33	Pennsylvania	Oconto	do	Laborer	
Champa, F	26	Canada	Albion	do	Engineer	
Cheeschrough, H	27	New York	Oconto	do	Farmer	
Cusswauac, M	18	Wisconsin	Sparta	do	Hunter	Transferred to Co. F June 2, '65.
Crocker, H	29	Ohio	Pensaukee	do	Farmer	
Delano, E	24	New York	Lima	do	do	
Elston, G W	18	Penn	Vermont	do	do	
Everson, John	21	Norway	Lima	do	do	
Flint, C F	18	New York	Cross Plains	do	do	
Grant, J W	57	Kentucky	Dunkirk	do	do	
Grow, Nathaniel	19	New York	Vermont	do	do	Wounded April 2, 1865.
Grove, M A	44	Norway	Oconto	do	do	App'd Corp. Nov. 21, 1864.
Glynn, J A		Ireland		do	do	

COMPANY G.—[CONTINUED.]

NAMES.	AGE.	WHERE BORN.	RESIDENCE.		OCCUPATION.	REMARKS.
Greenwood, Mr	25	Wisconsin	Green Bay	Wis	Farmer	Wounded April 2, 1865.
Gardner, I	37	Canada	Pensaukee	do	Laborer	Transf'd to Co. F, June 2, 1865.
Haring, Thos	35	New York		do	do	Deserted at Camp Randall July 28th, 1864.
Hamilton, J	22	Michigan			Lumberman	Bounty Jumper. Deserted at Camp Randall Sept. 21st, '64.
Harned, D M	19	Ohio	Union,	Wis	Farmer	Bruised by shell, Oct. 27, 1864, [at Hatcher's Run.
Hill, Welcome	43	New York	Albion,	do	do	
Hanson, Hans	30	Norway	Perry,	do	do	
Horsfall, Jas	35	England	Linn,	do	Shoemaker	
Huffman, G W	29	Ohio	do	do	Farmer	
Hills, O N	35	New York	do	do	do	Promoted Corporal Feb. 20, '65.
Harrison, F W	27	England	Albion,	do	do	Wounded in wrist April 2, 1865, and died soon after.
Hayacs, Wm	37	do	Cross Plains,	do	do	
Hackett, J	43	New York	Freedom	do	Farmer	
James, M	18	Canada	Lake Mills,	do	Laborer	
Kelley, Jas	23	Penn	Pensaukee,	do	Farmer	Wounded in foot, Feb. 16, '65. [Foot amputated same day.
Marzke, P A	19	Germany	Linn	do	do	
Morgan, John	42	Wales	Albion,	do	do	
Murphy, Pat	18	New York	Milton,	do	do	
Millard, A	24	do	Johnstown	do	Lumberman	
McCall, Chas	35	do	Oconto,	do	Farmer	Deserted Camp Randall, August 20, 1861.
Miller, Geo	23	Penn			Farmer	

Name	Age	Where born	Residence	Wis	Occupation	Remarks
Nippert, M T	29	Ohio	Freedom	do	Farmer	
Nelson, Henry	22	Norway	Blue Mounds	do	do	
Opsal, H O	30	Norway	Vermont	do	do	
Phillips, Wm	35	New York	Waterloo	do	do	Died in 9th Corps Hospital, City [Point, Va., Nov. 23, 1864.
Prothers, Wm	17	Indiana	Baraboo	do	do	
Pierson, Thos	24	Canada W	Oconto	do	Printer	
Patterson, D C	27	New York	do	do	Farmer	Wounded April 2d, 1865, and died same day.
Paige, S	18	Vermont	Stiles	do		Transferred to Co. F, June 2, '65
Ryan, M	18	do	Milwaukee	do	Sailor	
Rabe, Henry	35	Germany	Stiles	do	Lumberman	
Rice, R F	37	Vermont	Pensaukee	do	Farmer	
Rousseau, A E	20	Wisconsin	Green Bay	do	do	
Slater, J	29	England	Albion	do	do	
Slater, Wm	29	do	do	do	do	
Stiles, B F	31	New York	Waterloo	do	do	
Steinford, C	19	Prussia	do	do	do	
Thomas, O	24	New York	Lima Center	do	do	
Truckey, E B	19	Wisconsin	Green Bay	do	do	
Thwing, H	40	New York	Dunkirk	do	do	Nerve of right eye paralyzed by the bursting of a shell, Dec. 23, 1864.
Vance, H	22	New York	Koshkonong	do	do	
Vanetten, W H	38	do			do	Des. at Camp Randall, Sept. 18, [1864.
Webb, C T	30	New York	Lima	do	do	
Wells, Fred	18	England	Albion	do	do	
White, John	18	do	Milwaukee	do	Sailor	Transferred to Co. F, June 2, '65

T

COMPANY II.—MUSTERED OUT JULY 25TH, 1865.

NAMES.	AGE.	WHERE BORN.	RESIDENCE.	OCCUPATION.	REMARKS.
SERGEANTS.					
1st William Adams	29	Pennsylvania	Cadiz	Farmer	Promoted to 2d Lieut. Jan. 14, [1865.
2d J B Shank, Jr	23	do	Monroe	Clerk	
3d Harris Pool	41	Ohio	do	Blacksmith	
4th J A Bailey	31	Illinois	do	Farmer	
5th George P White	28	New York		do	
CORPORALS.					
John A Ford	29	Indiana	Monroe	Wis Farmer	Wounded April 2, 1865. Right leg amputated.
John G Saunders	33	Pennsylvania	Cadiz	do	Wounded April 2, 1865.
Wm R Hawkins	18	Indiana	Clarno	do	Killed April 2, 1865.
George W Thorp	22	Wisconsin	do	do	Promoted to 1st Serg't Feb. 1, '65
Joseph Snyder	21	Indiana	do	do	Died at City Point, Va., Dec 15, 1864.
PRIVATES.					
John C Jordan	25	Maine	Mt. Pleasant	do	Accidentally wounded in foot [Nov. 19, 1864.
Chambers V Musser	30	Pennsylvania	Rock Grove	Ill	Reduced to the ranks Sep. 21, '65
William Wallace	24	Ireland	Exeter	Wis	
Austin, Martin	43	New York	Cadiz	Wis Mechanic	Drummer in Regimental Band.
Baxter, A B	21	Vermont	Mt. Pleasant	Farmer	Wounded Oct. 28, 1864. Hand
Brown, Wm H	37	Pennsylvania	Monroe	do	[amputated. Dis. Dec. 17, '64.
Bees, Wm	30	N Hampshire	Clarno	do	Basket-maker

Name	Age	Born	Town	State	Occupation	Remarks
Booher, J J	18	Ohio	Mt. Pleasant	do	Farmer	Dis. for disability Dec. 22, '64.
Blanchard, C	17	do	do	do	do	
Bailey, J	21	Wisconsin	Sylvester	do	do	
Brown, John	39	England	Richland	do	do	
Corey, J W	18	Illinois	Monroe	do	do	
Campbell, Wm	25	Ohio	do	do	do	
Dexter, A W	37	N Hampshire	do	do	do	
Deetz, L	38	Pennsylvania	Cadiz	do	do	
Dolan, Martin	19	do	Monroe	do	do	
Dunaway, C	18	Ohio	do	do	do	Wounded April 2, 1865. Died May 8, 1865.
Dunn, Nelson	18	Wisconsin	do	do	do	Wounded April 2, 1865.
Davis, J	25	Pennsylvania	Adams	do	do	
Demery, W T	39	Ohio	Springfield	Nebraska	do	
Emerick, Wm	22	Pennsylvania	Charno	Wis	do	
Everett, D	30	Penn	Winslow,	Ill	Carpenter	
Everett, E J	20	do	do	do	Farmer	
Endriken, S	20	do	Adams,	Wis	do	
Frost, W J	17	Wisconsin	Sp'g Grove	do	Farmer	
Farlin, W H	30	Penn	Monroe,	do	Carpenter	
Fitzgerald, S	20	New York	Charno,	do	Farmer	
Hawkins, F M	19	Indiana	Charno,	do	do	
Johnson, M	21	Penn	Monroe,	do	Shoemaker	Discharged for disability.
Jewett, M	17	New York	Mt. Pleasant,	do	Farmer	Wounded April 2, 1865.
Killgore, E M	20	Indiana	Monroe,	do	Farmer	
Kellogg, J	19	New York	Beaver Dam,	do	Artist	
Kane, Henry	20	do	Monroe,	do	Farmer	Transferred from Co K, Oct. [25,] 1864.
Leahy, Jno	35	Ireland	Monroe,	do	Farmer	Appointed Corp'l Jan 4, 1865.
Land, Sidney	27	Illinois	Adams,	do	Farmer	do do do
Ligar, Auron	29	Penn	Monroe,	do	do	

COMPANY H.—[CONTINUED.]

NAMES.	AGE.	WHERE BORN.	RESIDENCE.		OCCUPATION.	REMARKS.
Lindley, O W	25	Illinois	Sylvester,	Wis	Farmer	Appointed Corp'l Feb. 1, '65. Wounded April 2, 1865. Left arm amputated.
Loveland, Thos	17	New York	Decatur,	do	do	Accidentally wounded on picket [line, Oct. 23d, 1864.
McMillan, J S	37	Ohio	Charno	do	do	
Miller, John	34	Germany	Monroe	do	do	
Miller, J S	20	Penn	do	do	do	
Miller, Emanuel	23	do	Cadiz	do	do	
McCardle, G R	22	Ohio	Charno	do	do	
Mears, John	18	Wisconsin	Monroe	do	do	
Marble, Ephraim	29	Penn	Winslow,	Ill	Sawyer	
Nash, Fred	41	England	Avon	Wis	Farmer	
O'Neal, Thos	18	Ireland	Charno	do	do	
Olmstead, E	19	Canada E	Auroraville	do	do	
Patterson, A W	18	New York	Mt. Pleasant	do	do	
Priece, Wm F	39	Prussia	Cadiz	do	do	
Riney, David	19	Wisconsin	Richland	do	do	
Randal, J N	27	Indiana	Monroe	do	do	Discharged for disability Jan. 14th, 1865.
Stubbs, Wm H	19	Penn	Jourdan	Wis	Farmer	
St Clair, R L	18	Michigan	Charno	do	do	
Sullivan, John	20	Ireland	do	do	do	
Sanders, J A	25	Penn	Cadiz	do	do	
Sanders, Wm D	20	do	do	do	do	
Staver, S W	25	do	Charno	do	do	

Name	Age	State	Town			Remarks
Snyder, T H	20	Illinois	do	do	do	Appointed Corp. Feb'y 20, 65.
Snyder, Elias	17	do	do	do	do	do do Jun. 4, 1865.
Small, Frank	18	Maine	Mt Pleasant	do	Clerk	
Satterlee, Robt	18	Wisconsin	Monroe	do	Farmer	
Start, S S	35	England	Adams	do	do	
Trogner, Geo	18	New York	Monroe	do	do	
Virtue, Stephen	28	Wisconsin	do	do	do	
Welch, Andrew	18	Wisconsin	Lloyd	do	do	
Wood, George J	23	Ohio	Sylvester	do	do	
West, Joseph	19	England	Monroe	do	do	
Wickersham, Q	28	Ohio	Adams	do	do	
Winkler, Andrew	30	Illinois	Monroe	do	do	
Wonderly, E D	18	Penn	Mt. Pleasant	do	do	
Wheeler, Nelson	33	New York	Sylvester	do	do	
Warren, Jno	39	Ohio	Cadiz	do	do	
Collins, Isaac	44	N Carolina	Newark Valley	do	do	Colored Cook.
Jomer, J A	26	Illinois	do	do	do	do do

COMPANY I.—MUSTERED OUT JUNE 2D, 1865.

NAMES.	AGE.	WHERE BORN.	RESIDENCE.	OCCUPATION.	REMARKS.
SERGEANTS.					
1st. E H Benham	24	Wisconsin	Janesville, Wis	Law Student	Wounded in Virginia, April 2,'65
2d. Jos. Terpening	36	New York	Perry, do	Farmer	Reduced to the ranks, Jan.31,'65
3d. David J Dann	24	New York	Waupun, do	Painter	
4th. Chas H Churchill,	21	New York	St Croix, do	Lumberman	Died in 1st Div., 9th A C hospital, Dec 17, 1864.
5th. Jas Licklighter	28	Ohio	Fond du Lac, do	Machinist	Promoted to 4th Sergt, Dec. 20, 1864. Promoted to 2d Sergt. Jan. 31, 1865.
CORPORALS.					
Jas Sheared	24	Canada	Winslow, Ill	Farmer	Promoted to Sergt. May 1, 1865.
H J Bennett	33	Mass	Martelle, Wis	do	[Wounded April 2, '65—heel.
J Kuykundall	19	Illinois	Buena Vista, do	do	
M Satten	40	Norway	Martell, do	do	Promoted to 5th Sergt. Jan. 31, [1865.. Wounded April 2, '65
Ed Rowley	40	Ireland	Fulton, do	Laborer	
James H Walters	31	Ohio	Rush River, do	Barber	Wounded April 2, 1865.
W B Brown	19	Vermont	Magnolia, do	Farmer	Promoted 6th Sergt. Dec. 20, 1864. Promoted to 4th Sergt. Jan. 31, 1865.
Andrew Addy	24	Scotland	Milton, do	Farmer	
PRIVATES.					
Arneson, A	80	Norway	Martell Wis	Farmer	Discharged for disability Dec. 7, [1864.
Andrews, James	40	New York	Waupaca do	do	

Name	Age	Nativity	Residence	State	Occupation	Remarks
Ballinger, A A	33	Ohio	Wayne	do	do	Killed April 2, 1865.
Battin, Wm	25	do	Washington	do	Blacksmith	
Blaisdell, A	18	Illinois	Diamond Bluff	do	Laborer	Wounded in head April 2, 1865.
Buttnell, G	24	Pennsylvania	Wayne	do	Farmer	Appointed Corp. May 1, 1865.
Bullis, A	32	New York	Milton Rock	do	do	Wounded in hand April 2, 1865.
Bullis, J	37	do	do	do	do	
Brown, John	25	Canada	Buena Vista	do	Laborer ?	
Campbell, F	36	Pennsylvania	Waupaca	do	Farmer	
Cursley, S H	27	Maine	N Centerville	do	Laborer	
Coosey, Pat	19	Canada	Johnstown	do	Farmer	
Cruse, E W	28	New York			Laborer	Slightly wounded in face April 2, 1865.
Cruse, John	23	Ireland	Elgerton	do	Laborer	Slightly wounded in back April 2, 1865.
Dunphy, Jas	20	Connecticut	Janesville,	do	do	Contusion wound of right hand, [April 2, 1865.
Dunn, Jno	34	Scotland	do	do	Farmer	
Drake, J P	23	New York,	Stockbridge,	do	do	
Dean, H E	25	Canada	Canada		Baker	
Emery, Cyrus	19	Massachusetts	St Croix Falls,	do	Farmer	
Endress, Fred	36	Germany	Ellsworth,	Wis	Farmer	
Francis, Jno W	18	Ohio	Janesville,	do	do	Des. Camp Randall Aug. 25, '64.
Ferguson, C B	20	Maine	Trimbell,	do	do	do do do 25, do
Frasier, Wm	41	Pennsylvania			do	
Frasier, Fraiser	25	do			do	
Goodsell, B	22	Vermont	St Croix Falls	do	do	Appointed Corporal Jan. 10, '65.
Heyerdahl, C	42	Norway	Martell	do	do	[Wounded on picket line April 2, 1865.
Henry, Lewis	19	Ohio	Buena Vista	do	do	
Henry, David	20	do	do	do	do	

COMPANY I.—[CONTINUED.]

NAMES.	AGE.	WHERE BORN.	RESIDENCE.	OCCUPATION.		REMARKS.
Howe, A H	29	Illinois	Cadiz	Wis	Farmer	Wounded in shoulder April 2,'65
Howe, T B	18	do	Winslow	Illinois	Carpenter	
Hunter, A	22	Penn	Warren	do	Farmer	
Hillstad, E A	18	Norway	Black Earth,	Wis	Farmer	Killed by sharpshooter Dec. 27, [1864, while on picket.
Kline, R J	18	Wisconsin			do	
Leach, B L	37	New York	Trimbell	do	Cooper	
Lynch, Brien	36	Ireland	Edgerton,	do	Laborer	
Lyons, Jas	40	do	do	do	Farmer	
McWain, H	22	Canada	Whitby, Canada W		Teamster	
McInto-h E	18	Iowa	St Croix,	Wis	Farmer	
Mullen, M	18	Ireland	Harmony	do	Laborer	
Mann, John	37	New York			Farmer	
Mon-or, L	30	Maine	Hortonville	do	Carpenter	Struck by fragment of shell April 2d 1865.
Mooney, Patrick	35	Ireland	Fulton	do	Brickmaker	Deserted Camp Randall Aug. 20th, 1864.
Martin, Jas	23	Canada			Sailor	Deserted Camp Randall Aug. 22, 1864.
McCoy, Jno	22	Maine			Painter	
Oleson, B	25	Norway	Martell	Wis	Farmer	
Otis, Jas F	20	Penn	Trimbell	do	do	
Owens, John	41	Norway	Martell,	do	Blacksmith	
Oviatt, C B	16	Wisconsin	Albion	do	Farmer	
Peterson, P	38	Norway	Martell	do	do	
Quigley, P M	23	Ireland	Fulton	do	Laborer	

Name	Age	Birthplace	Town		Occupation	Remarks
Rockwell, D J	25	New York	Wayne	Wis	Farmer	
Roxter, A C	18	Norway	Martell	do	Laborer	
Santimere, L	33	Pennsylvania	Trimbell	do	Farmer	
Simenson, M	38	Norway	Martell	do	do	
Smith, Wm	29	Austria	Oak Grove	do	do	Killed on picket duty Jan. 7, '65.
Setzer, M	24	Pennsylvania	Magnolia	do	do	
Stevens, Samuel	21	Ohio	Dodge County	do	do	
Stillman, A	32	New York	Fulton	do	do	
Stone, L R	22	Wisconsin	Wayne	do	do	
Sheard, Thomas	21	Canada	Winslow	do	do	
Sheard, Henry	18	do	do	do	do	
Seivert, L	23	France	Prescott	Wis	Carpenter	
Sischo, L	37	New York	Auburn	do	Farmer	
Stoddard, H F	19	do	Willow	do	do	Deserted from Camp Randall Sep't 12, 1864.
Swingle, A	20	Pennsylvania		do	Laborer	Deserted to the enemy Jun. 14, [1865.
Todd, D W	21	New Jersey	Milton	do	Hatter	
Tuttle, A	33	New York	Auburn	do	Farmer	
Vandyke, W O	17	Wisconsin	Janesville,	do	Farmer?	
Verley, B J	26	New York	Wiota	do	do	
Waye, Wm H	20	Illinois	Albion	do	do	
Williams, F T	17	New York	Trimbell	do	do	
Warth, H H	19	Wisconsin	St Croix Falls	do	Lumberman	
Wolf, Abraham	20	Germany	Ithica	do	Farmer	Wounded in leg and hand April 2, 1864.
Williams, Jos	26	England	Fulton	do	Brickmaker	
White, Chauncey	19	New York	Milton	do	Farmer	
Wells, P W	23	Illinois	Brushy Fork, Ill	do	do	
Whitcomb, S E	23	New York	Lowell	Wis	do	
Weaver, Fred	20	Germany			Drayman	

COMPANY K.—MUSTERED OUT JUNE 2D, 1865.

NAMES.	AGE.	WHERE BORN.	RESIDENCE.	OCCUPATION.	REMARKS.
SERGEANTS.					
1st. Aug. S Rogers	31	N.Hampshire	Marion,	Wis	Farmer	Discharged for disability, Nov. 25, 1864.
2d. Wm E Gibbens	30	England	White Creek	do	Shoemaker	Promoted 1st Sergt Nov.26, '64.
3d. L W Wetherbee		Indiana	do	do	Miller	Promoted 2d Sergt Nov.26, '64. Wounded April 2, 1865.
4th. Albert S Prouty	34	Mass	New Haven	do	Farmer	Promoted 3d Sergt Nov.26, '64,
5th. William Myers	35	New York	White Creek	do	Millwright	Promoted 4th Sergt Nov. 27, '64.
CORPORALS.					
And. B Bronson	23	Wisconsin	Rome,	Wis	Lumberman	Wounded April 2, 1865. Leg Amputated.
Chas N Bullis	20	Ohio	Dell Prairie,	do	Farmer	Transferred to Co. C, June 2, '65.
Andrew J Fish	23	New York	Jackson,	do	do	Wounded April 2, 1865.
Thos R Freeman	33	Vermont	Springville,	do	do	
Wm H Quaw	35	New York	Friendship,	do	do	
James Chalmers	40	Scotland	do	do	Merchant	
Elisha B Redfield	37	Vermont	Adams.	do	Joiner	
Chas H Mosher	23	New York	White Creek	do	Farmer	Promoted 5th Sergt, Nov. 26, 1864. Wounded slightly, April 2, 1865.

MUSICIANS.

Name	Age	Birthplace	Residence	State	Occupation	Remarks
James M Harrison	32	New York	Friendship,	Wis	Musician	Transferred to Co C June 2, '65.
Jacob C Stevens		New York	Monroe,	do	Farmer	

PRIVATES.

Name	Age	Birthplace	Residence	State	Occupation	Remarks
Alverson, Phineas S	29	New York	Harmony,	Wis	Farmer	
Bidwell, Jacob W	18	do	Easton,	do	do	Wounded slightly April 2, 1865.
Bidwell, James A	27	do	do	do	do	Discharged for disability Jan'y [1865.
Brown, Amos	35	do	do	do	Carpenter	
Brown, Lewis	20	Germany	Columbus	do	Farmer	
Burnham, Theo G	21	New York	Jackson	do	do	
Babcock, Darick	37	do	Easton	do	do	
Burdick, Joel Q	39	do	do	do	do	Died in McDougall Hospital Nov. [14, 1865, of chronic diarrhœa.
Clark, Daniel	26	do		do	do	
Colburn, Sherman	40	Vermont	Springville	do	Currier	
Chapman, Geo W	18	West Indies	Monroe	do	Lumberman	
Cook, Wm H	23	New York	Quincy	do	Farmer	
Carning, Wm	27	Maine	Strong's Prairie	do	do	
Clark, Geo C	42	New York	Portage	do	do	
Davis, Thomas	33	England	Lincoln	do	do	
Eddy, Wm A	22	New York	Easton	do	Wagonmaker	
Frazier, L F	19	do	Oxford	do	Farmer	
Frazier, B A	18	do	do	do	do	Wounded in hand April 2, 1865.
Frazier, L	28	New York	Oxford	do	do	
Fields, N A	17	Wisconsin	Adams	do	do	
Fitch, J P	44	New York	New Haven	do	do	
Grier, Abraham	43	England	Jackson	do	do	
Hines, Dennis	18	Wisconsin	Dell Prairie	do	Raftsman	Wounded in knee April 2, 1865.

COMPANY K.—[CONTINUED.]

NAMES.	AGE.	WHERE BORN.	RESIDENCE.		OCCUPATION.	REMARKS.
Harrington, George	30	New York	Easton	Wis	Farmer'	
Haskins, Leroy	17	do	Preston	do	do	
Hatch, J K P	19	do	Dell Prairie	do		
Harrington, Phillip	21	Connecticut	Quincy	do	Lumberman	Discharged for disability.
Hakes, Byron	25	New York	White Creek	do	Farmer	Died in Harewood Hospital Nov. [1, 1864.
Harrison, George	24	England	Strong's Pra	do	Merchant	
Haskins, D S	21	New York	Colona	do	Farmer	
Hammond, Henry,	40	New York	Friendship	do	Lumberman	
Hardine, Theodore	25	Maine	Big Flats	do	Farmer	Wounded by shell March 4, 65.
Jefferson, James	20	Canada	Monroe	do	do	
Johnson, Lars	37	Norway	Armenia	do	do	
Jents, F M	30	New York	White Creek	do	Mechanic	
Johnson, C	44	New Jersey	Springville	do	Farmer	
Knapp, H H	16	Ohio	Preston	do	do	
Keyes, Charles	24	New York	Strong's Pra	do	Lumberman	
Kane, Henry	20	do	Monroe	do	Farmer	
Litchfield, James	30	Vermont	Easton	do	Blacksmith	Transferred to Co. H, Oct. 25, [1864.
Lawrence, H T	20	Wisconsin			Farmer	Deserted at Madison, Sept. 22, [1864.
Macumber, Wesley	29	New York	Springville	do	do	
Millard, Cassius F	17	do	Preston	do	do	
Mix, Franklin	17	Wisconsin	Richfield	do	do	
Marble, N J	39	New York	Easton	do	do	
Manning, P	44	Ireland	Milwaukee	do	Coachman	
O Neil, Thomas	44	do	Oregon	do	Farmer	
Obert, Francis M	18	Wisconsin	Union	do	do	

Name	Age	Birthplace	Residence		Occupation	Remarks
Odell, Jno A	32	Canada	Strong's Pra	do	Lumberman	Colonel's Orderly.
Perkins, Wm E	39	Vermont	White Creek	do	Shoemaker	Accidentally shot while on picket, Oct. 13, 1864, and died next day.
Parker, Ira L	22	New York	Marion	do	Farmer	
Parkins, Thos W	20	England	Richfield	do	do	Promoted to Corporal Nov. 26, [1864.
Pells, David	16	Wisconsin	do	do	do	Wounded April 2, 1865.
Parker, A R	28	Vermont	Marion	do	do	
Reeves, Anson	34	New York	Springville	do	Miller	Wounded April 2, 1865.
Ripley, I A	21	do	do	do	Farmer	Died in Armory Square Hospital [December 16, 1864.
Ryder, Chas W	43	New York	Big Flats	do	Blacksmith	
Scott, Otis B	40	Vermont	Easton	do	Farmer	
Stevens, Jacob C	44	New York	Monroe	do	do	
Sormerud, S H	30	Norway	Strong's Pra	do	do	
Simpson, Phillip	27	New York	NewarkValley	do	do	
Slater, E L	19	do	Springville	do	do	Died at home Sept. 3, 1864.
Thomas, J W	21	Indiana	Jackson	do	do	
Townsend, John	22	New York	Dell Prairie	do	Minister	
Thompson, Reuben	36	do	White Creek	do	Farmer	Wounded in cheek April 2, '65.
Vantassel, Wm R	20	do	Adams	do	do	Wounded in leg April 2, '65.
Van Wie, Nelson	33	do	Easton	do	do	
Vrooman, Myron	22	Penn	Jackson	do	do	Wounded slightly April 2, '65.
Walrath, Daniel	21	New York	White Creek	do	do	
Wright, Willard A	20	do	Friendship	do	do	
Warwick, William	36	Ohio	Marion	do	do	Severely wounded in thigh April 2, '65. Discharged July 5, '64.
Winterstein, Jacob	33	do	Springville	do	do	Des. at Camp Randall Aug. 17, '64
Winchell, Clinton D	19	Wisconsin	do	do	Lumberman	do
Dudley, Patrick	34	Ireland	Milwaukee,	do	Hostler	do
Killbourne, Michael	22	do	do	do	Laborer	do

COMPANY K.—[CONTINUED.]

NAMES.	AGE.	WHERE BORN.	RESIDENCE.		OCCUPATION.	REMARKS.			
Keeler, Ed	23	Ireland	Milwaukee,	Wis	Teamster	Des. Camp Randall Aug. 17, '64.			
Kinney, Jos	20	Canada	do	do	Farmer	do	do	do	do
Moley, James	23	do	do	do	Boatman	do	do	do	do
Montgomery, James	24	Scotland	do	do	Clerk	do	do	do	do
Reed, Rudolph	24	Great Britain	do	do	Hackman	do	do	do	do

F 8 3 4 9 . ? 8 ? 5

ERRATA.

On page 25, first line of second paragraph, for *cannister* read *canister*.

On page 128, first line of second paragraph, for 14th read 4th.

On page 158, third line of third paragraph and second line of last paragraph, for *Pearson* read *Pierson*.

On page 217, fifth line from bottom, for 4865 read 1865.

On page 222, fifth line, for *Albree* read *Albee*.

On page 223, ninth line from top, for 1863 read 1864.